SCHIRMER'S LIBRARY OF MUSICAL CLASSICS

Vol. 1037

WALTER MACFARREN

Scale and Arpeggio Manual

For the Piano

G. SCHIRMER, Inc.

DISTRIBUTED BY

HAL•LEONARD
CORPORATION

7777 W. BLUEMOUND RD. P.O. BOX 13819 MILWAUKEE, WI 53213

DIRECTIONS FOR PRACTICE

1. SCALES—both Diatonic and Chromatic—should at first be limited to one octave; then extended to two and three octaves and, subsequently, to the whole range of the keyboard. The student should acquire the habit of commencing scales from the higher as well as the lower end of the keyboard, and should play them in similar and in contrary motion, commencing sometimes with both hands in the centre, and at other times with the hands at the extreme ends. He should also practise them *staccato* (from the finger as well as the wrist) and *legato*.

2. The Arbitrary or Melodic Minor Scales should *not* be practised in contrary motion, in consequence of the harsh effect induced thereby, but should be commenced at the higher as well as the lower end of the keyboard.

3. The Chromatic Scale is given with two methods of fingering, the first of which should be mastered before the second is attempted. It should be commenced at the higher as well as the lower end of the keyboard, and should be practised *staccato* (from the finger as well as the wrist) and *legato*.

4. ARPEGGIOS of Common Chords, Dominant Sevenths and Diminished Sevenths, should at first be limited to one octave and subsequently extended to two and three octaves. They should also be practised in contrary as well as in similar motion, commencing at the extreme ends as well as in the middle of the keyboard. They should likewise be played *staccato* (from the finger as well as the wrist) and *legato*.

5. Scales in double thirds and double sixths should *not* be practised in contrary motion until the fingering has been mastered. They should be commenced at the higher as well as the lower end of the keyboard, and played *staccato* as well as *legato*.

6. Scales in double octaves should be practised *legato* as well as *staccato;* when *legato*, with the fourth finger on the black notes, and the wrist slightly depressed; when *staccato*, with the fifth finger on every octave, lifting the hand lightly from the wrist. They should also be practised in contrary and similar motion.

7. *Slow* practice is GOLDEN; *quick* practice is LEADEN.

8. This edition includes an APPENDIX, beginning on page 60, in which the rules for practice set down in the foregoing remarks are more fully illustrated than hitherto. It also contains examples of Arpeggios of Chords not previously set forth in the Manual, and the Arbitrary or Melodic Minor Scales in thirds and sixths.

9. In the APPENDIX every form of Arpeggio, as well as of Scale, in similar and contrary motion, is fully exemplified in the key of C, and the student is advised to apply these in succession to all the other keys.

WALTER MACFARREN.

The Comprehensive Scale and Arpeggio Manual

DIATONIC SCALES

Scale of C

Walter Macfarren

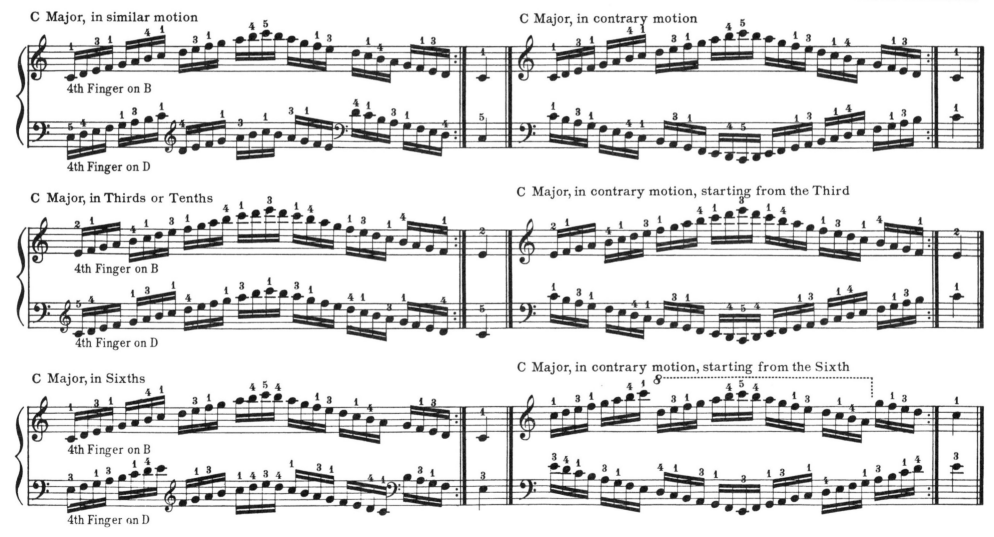

Copyright, 1915, by G. Schirmer, Inc.
Printed in the U. S. A.

Harmonic C Minor, in similar motion

Harmonic C Minor, in contrary motion

4th Finger on B♮

4th Finger on D

Harmonic C Minor, in Thirds or Tenths

Harmonic C Minor, in contrary motion starting from the Third

4th Finger on B♮

4th Finger on D

Harmonic C Minor, in Sixths

Harmonic C Minor, in contrary motion starting from the Sixth

4th Finger on B♮

4th Finger on D

Arbitrary or Melodic C Minor, in similar motion, commencing from the lowest and also from the highest note

4th Finger on B♮ ascending and B♭ descending

4th Finger on D

Scale of G

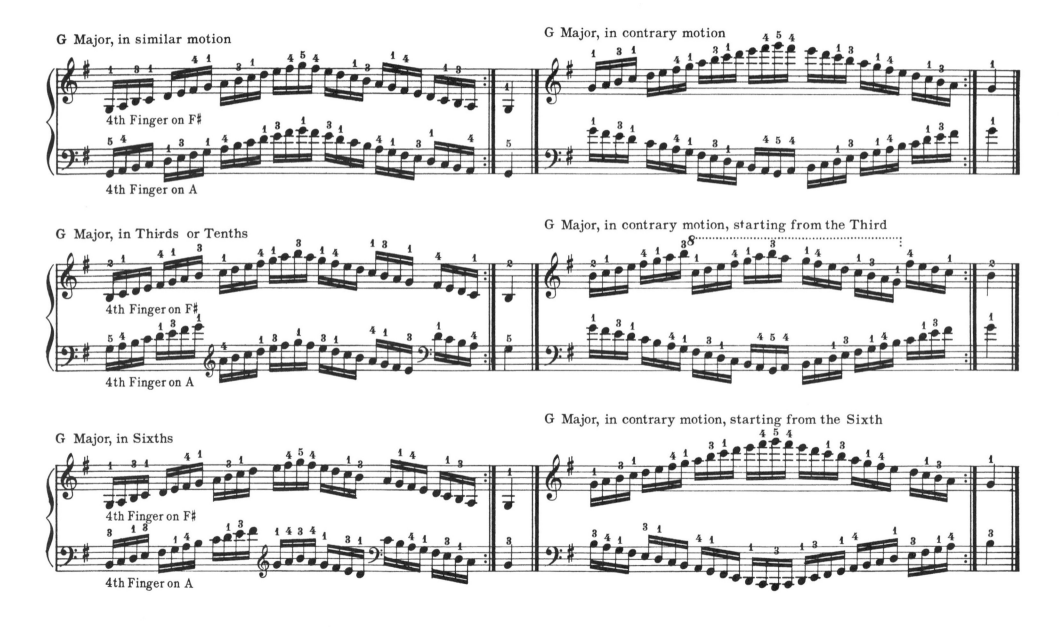

Harmonic G Minor, in similar motion

Harmonic G Minor, in contrary motion

Harmonic G Minor, in Thirds or Tenths

Harmonic G Minor, in contrary motion, starting from the Third

Harmonic G Minor, in Sixths

Harmonic G Minor, in contrary motion, starting from the Sixth

Arbitrary or Melodic G Minor, in similar motion, commencing from the lowest and also from the highest note

4th Finger on F♯

4th Finger on A

4th Finger on F♯

4th Finger on A

4th Finger on F♯

4th Finger on A

4th Finger on F♯ ascending and F♮ descending

4th Finger on A

Scale of D

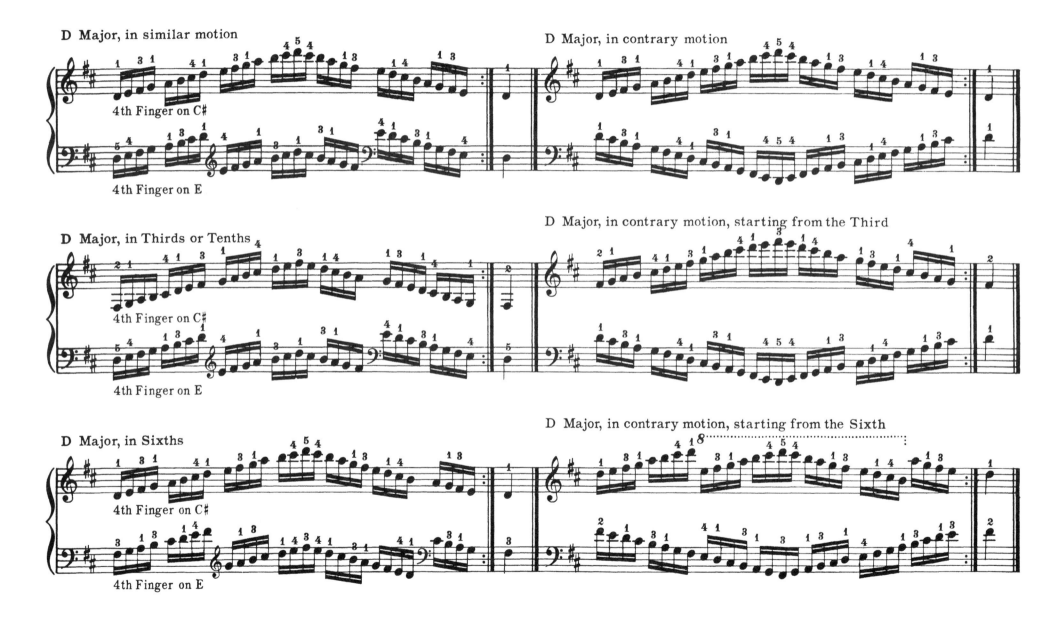

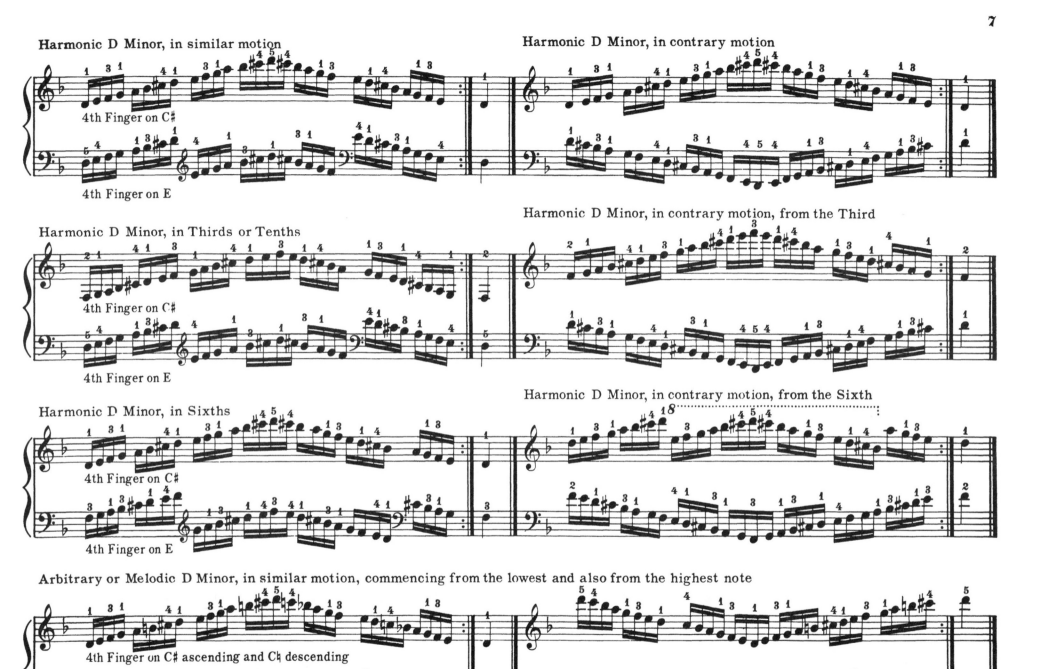

Harmonic D Minor, in similar motion

4th Finger on C♯

4th Finger on E

Harmonic D Minor, in contrary motion

Harmonic D Minor, in Thirds or Tenths

4th Finger on C♯

4th Finger on E

Harmonic D Minor, in contrary motion, from the Third

Harmonic D Minor, in Sixths

4th Finger on C♯

4th Finger on E

Harmonic D Minor, in contrary motion, from the Sixth

Arbitrary or Melodic D Minor, in similar motion, commencing from the lowest and also from the highest note

4th Finger on C♯ ascending and C♮ descending

4th Finger on E

25367

Scale of A

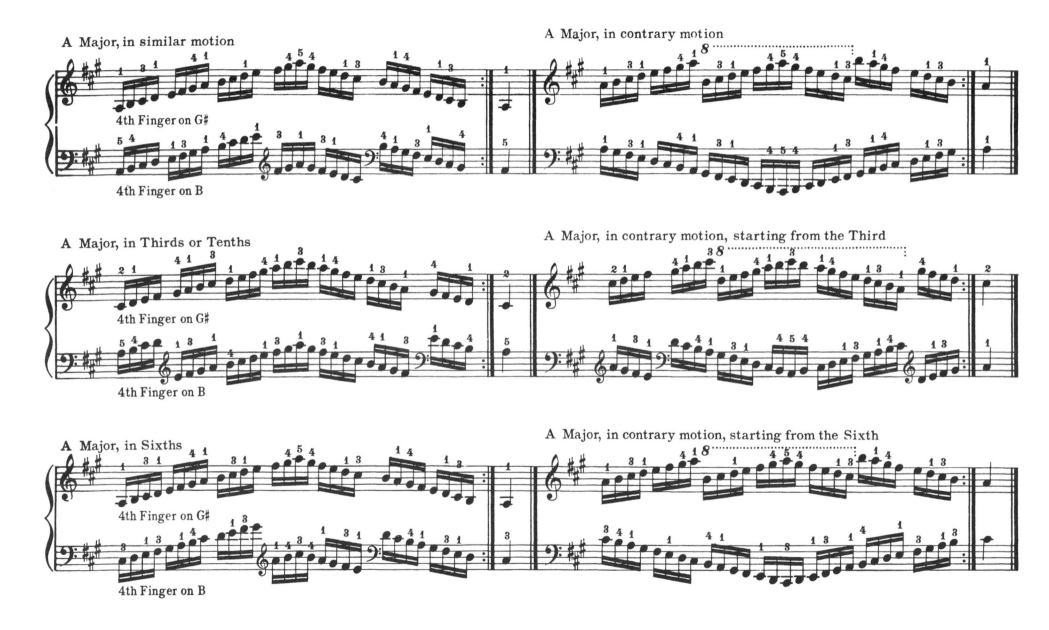

A Major, in similar motion

4th Finger on G♯

4th Finger on B

A Major, in contrary motion

A Major, in Thirds or Tenths

4th Finger on G♯

4th Finger on B

A Major, in contrary motion, starting from the Third

A Major, in Sixths

4th Finger on G♯

4th Finger on B

A Major, in contrary motion, starting from the Sixth

Harmonic A Minor, in similar motion

Harmonic A Minor, in contrary motion

4th Finger on G#

4th Finger on B

Harmonic A Minor, in Thirds or Tenths

Harmonic A Minor, in contrary motion, starting from the Third

4th Finger on G#

4th Finger on B

Harmonic A Minor, in Sixths

Harmonic A Minor, in contrary motion, starting from the Sixth

4th Finger on G#

4th Finger on B

Arbitrary or Melodic A Minor, in similar motion, commencing from the lowest and also from the highest note

4th Finger on G# ascending and G♮ descending

4th Finger on B

Scale of E

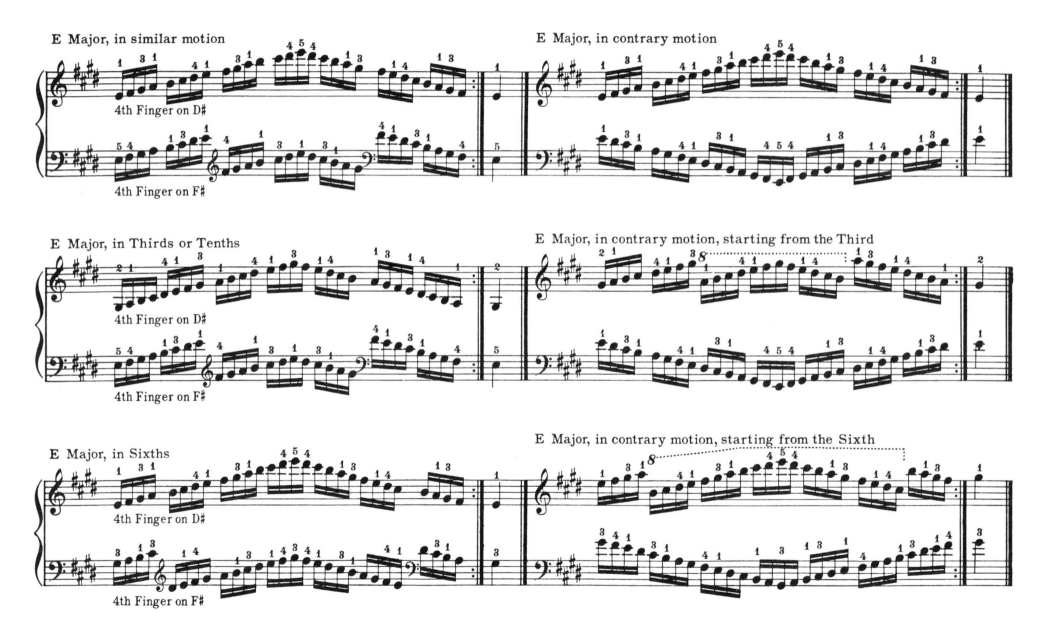

Harmonic E Minor, in similar motion

Harmonic E Minor, in contrary motion

Harmonic E Minor, in Thirds or Tenths

Harmonic E Minor, in contrary motion, starting from the Third

Harmonic E Minor, in Sixths

Harmonic E Minor, in contrary motion, starting from the Sixth

4th Finger on D♯

4th Finger on F♯

Arbitrary or Melodic E Minor, in similar motion, commencing from the lowest and also from the highest note

4th Finger on D♯ ascending and D♮ descending

4th Finger on F♯

25367

Scale of B

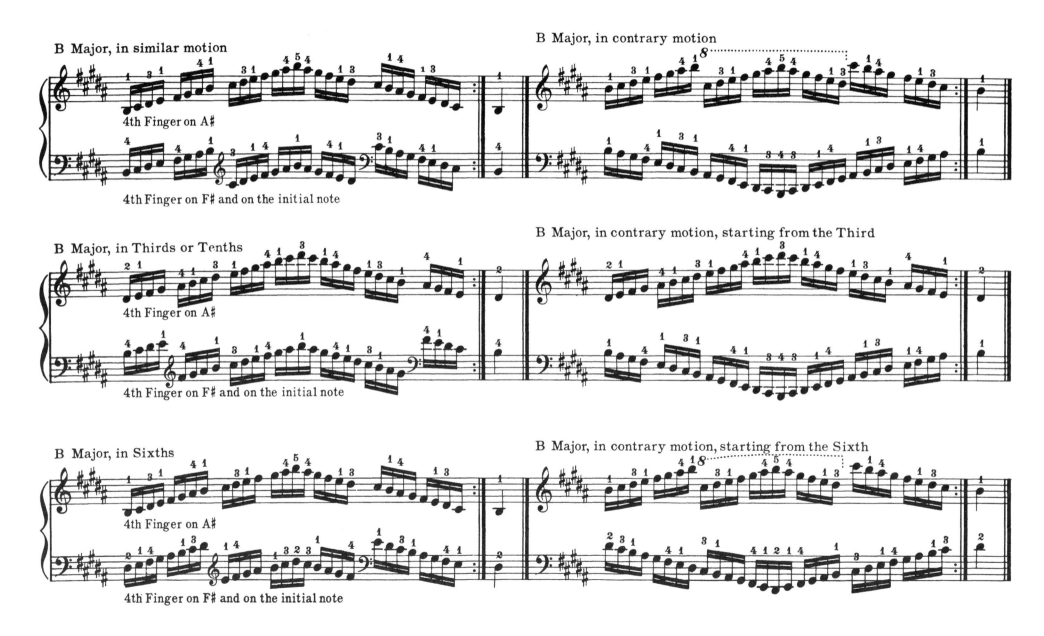

B Major, in similar motion

4th Finger on A♯

4th Finger on F♯ and on the initial note

B Major, in contrary motion

B Major, in Thirds or Tenths

4th Finger on A♯

4th Finger on F♯ and on the initial note

B Major, in contrary motion, starting from the Third

B Major, in Sixths

4th Finger on A♯

4th Finger on F♯ and on the initial note

B Major, in contrary motion, starting from the Sixth

Harmonic B Minor, in similar motion

Harmonic B Minor, in contrary motion

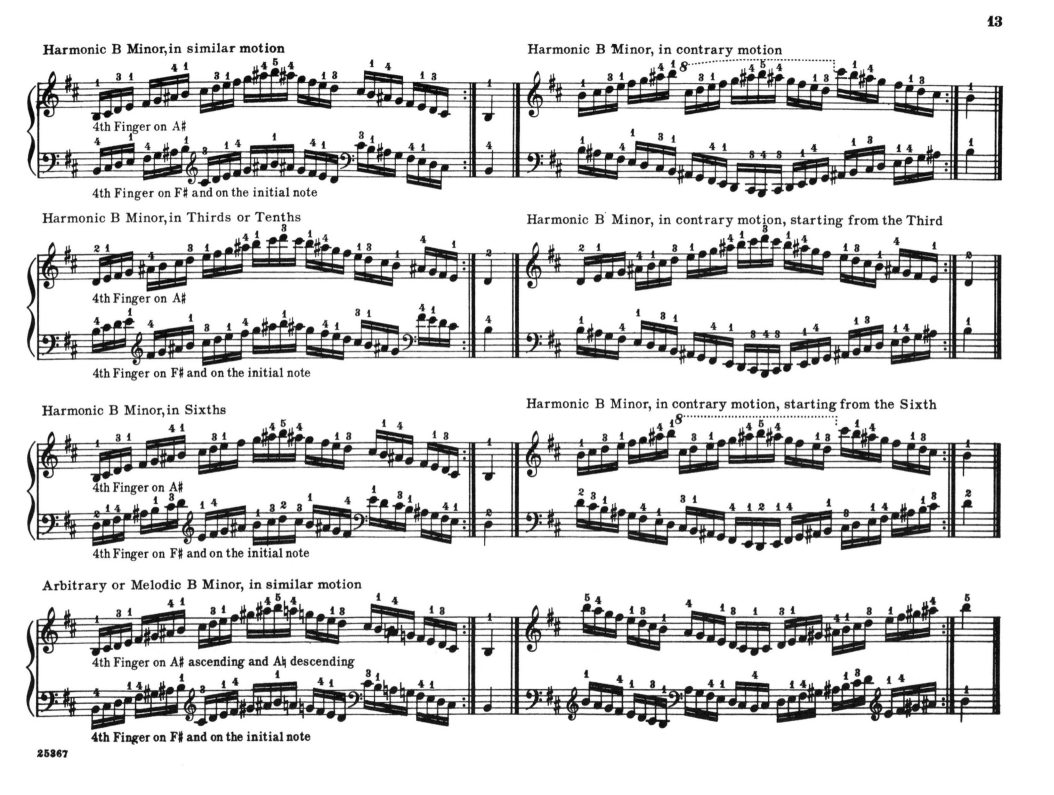

4th Finger on A#

4th Finger on F# and on the initial note

Harmonic B Minor, in Thirds or Tenths

Harmonic B Minor, in contrary motion, starting from the Third

4th Finger on A#

4th Finger on F# and on the initial note

Harmonic B Minor, in Sixths

Harmonic B Minor, in contrary motion, starting from the Sixth

4th Finger on A#

4th Finger on F# and on the initial note

Arbitrary or Melodic B Minor, in similar motion

4th Finger on A# ascending and A♮ descending

4th Finger on F# and on the initial note

Scale of F Sharp

(Enharmonic Equivalent G♭)

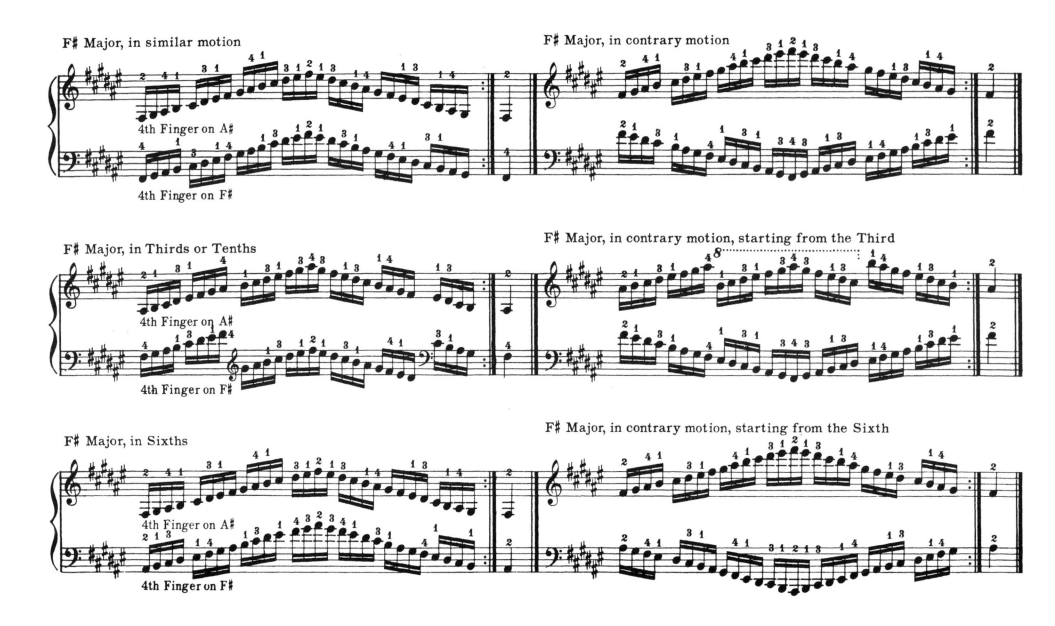

F♯ Major, in similar motion

4th Finger on A♯

4th Finger on F♯

F♯ Major, in contrary motion

F♯ Major, in Thirds or Tenths

4th Finger on A♯

4th Finger on F♯

F♯ Major, in contrary motion, starting from the Third

F♯ Major, in Sixths

4th Finger on A♯

4th Finger on F♯

F♯ Major, in contrary motion, starting from the Sixth

Harmonic F# Minor, in similar motion

Harmonic F# Minor, in contrary motion

4th Finger on G#

4th Finger on F#

Harmonic F# Minor, in Thirds or Tenths

Harmonic F# Minor, in contrary motion, starting from the Third

4th Finger on G#

4th Finger on F#

Harmonic F# Minor, in Sixths

Harmonic F# Minor, in contrary motion, starting from the Sixth

4th Finger on G#

4th Finger on F#

Arbitrary or Melodic F# Minor, in similar motion

4th Finger on D# ascending and G# descending

4th Finger on F#

25367

Scale of C Sharp

(Enharmonic Equivalent D♭)

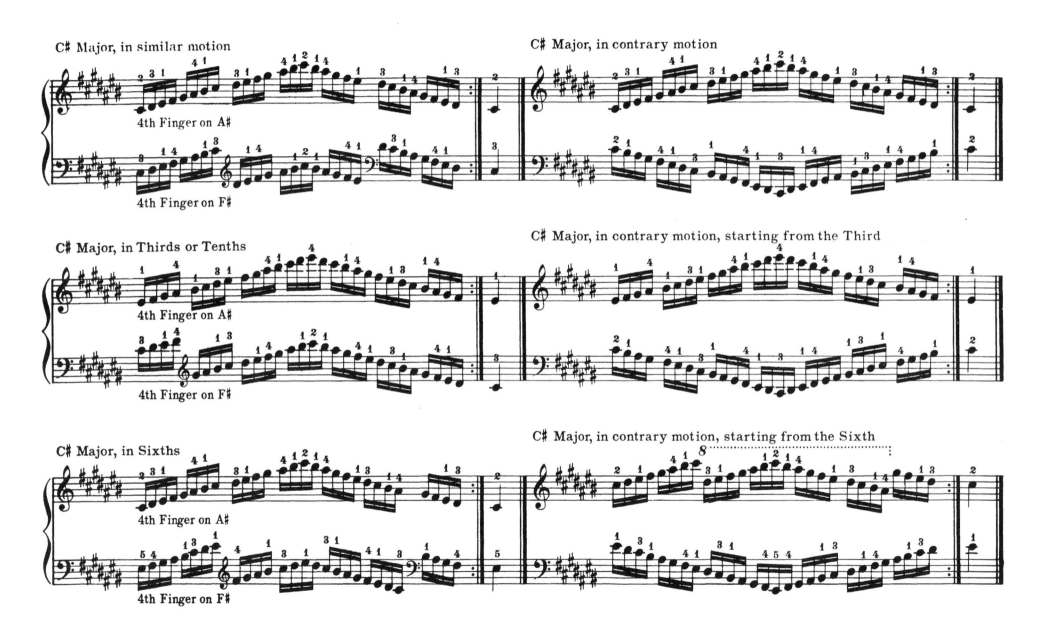

C♯ Major, in similar motion

4th Finger on A♯

4th Finger on F♯

C♯ Major, in contrary motion

C♯ Major, in Thirds or Tenths

4th Finger on A♯

4th Finger on F♯

C♯ Major, in contrary motion, starting from the Third

C♯ Major, in Sixths

4th Finger on A♯

4th Finger on F♯

C♯ Major, in contrary motion, starting from the Sixth

Harmonic C♯ Minor, in similar motion

Harmonic C♯ Minor, in contrary motion

Harmonic C♯ Minor, in Thirds or Tenths

Harmonic C♯ Minor, in contrary motion, starting from the Third

Harmonic C♯ Minor, in Sixths

Harmonic C♯ Minor, in contrary motion, starting from the Sixth

Arbitrary or Melodic C♯ Minor, in similar motion

4th Finger on D♯

4th Finger on F♯

4th Finger on A♯ ascending and D♯ descending

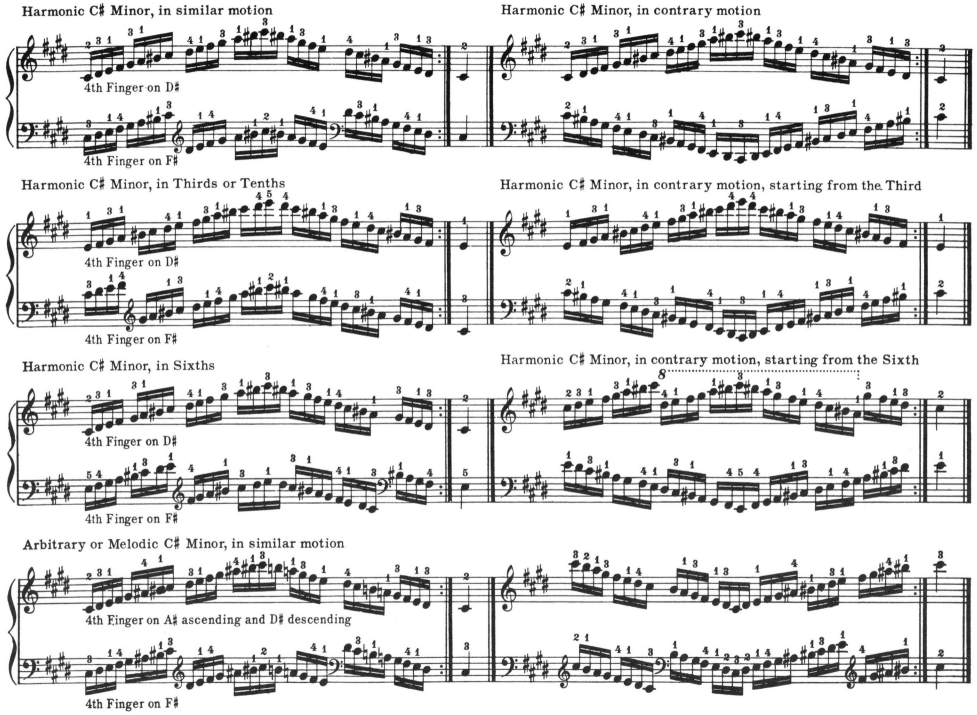

Scale of A Flat

(Enharmonic Equivalent G♯)

Ab Major, in similar motion

4th Finger on B♭

4th Finger on D♭

Ab Major, in contrary motion

Ab Major, in Thirds or Tenths

4th Finger on B♭

4th Finger on D♭

Ab Major, in contrary motion, starting from the Third

Ab Major, in Sixths

4th Finger on B♭

4th Finger on D♭

Ab Major, in contrary motion, starting from the Sixth

Harmonic Ab Minor (Enharmonic G# minor), in similar motion

Harmonic Ab Minor, in contrary motion

4th Finger on Bb

4th Finger on Db

Harmonic Ab Minor, in Thirds or Tenths

Harmonic Ab Minor, in contrary motion, starting from the Third

4th Finger on Bb

4th Finger on Db

Harmonic Ab Minor, in Sixths

Harmonic Ab Minor, in contrary motion, starting from the Sixth

4th Finger on Bb

4th Finger on Db

Arbitrary or Melodic Ab Minor, in similar motion

4th Finger on Bb

4th Finger on Db ascending and Gb descending

Scale of E Flat

(Enharmonic Equivalent D♯)

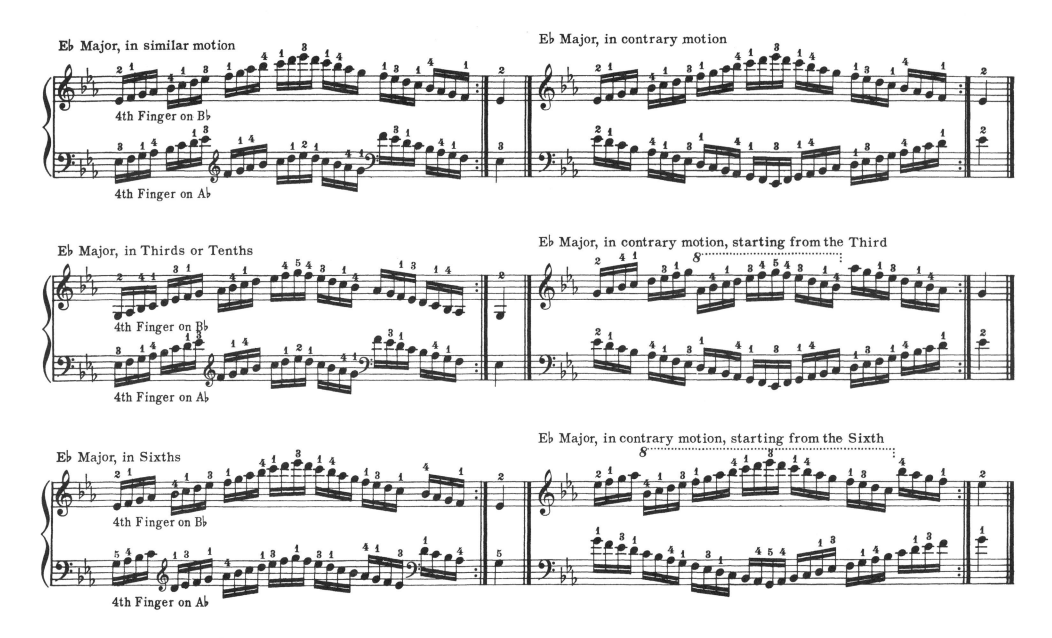

Harmonic E♭ Minor, in similar motion

Harmonic E♭ Minor, in contrary motion

Harmonic E♭ Minor, in Thirds or Tenths

Harmonic E♭ Minor, in contrary motion, starting from the Third

Harmonic E♭ Minor, in Sixths

Harmonic E♭ Minor, in contrary motion, starting from the Sixth

Arbitrary or Melodic E♭ Minor, in similar motion

4th Finger on B♭

4th Finger on G♭

Scale of B Flat

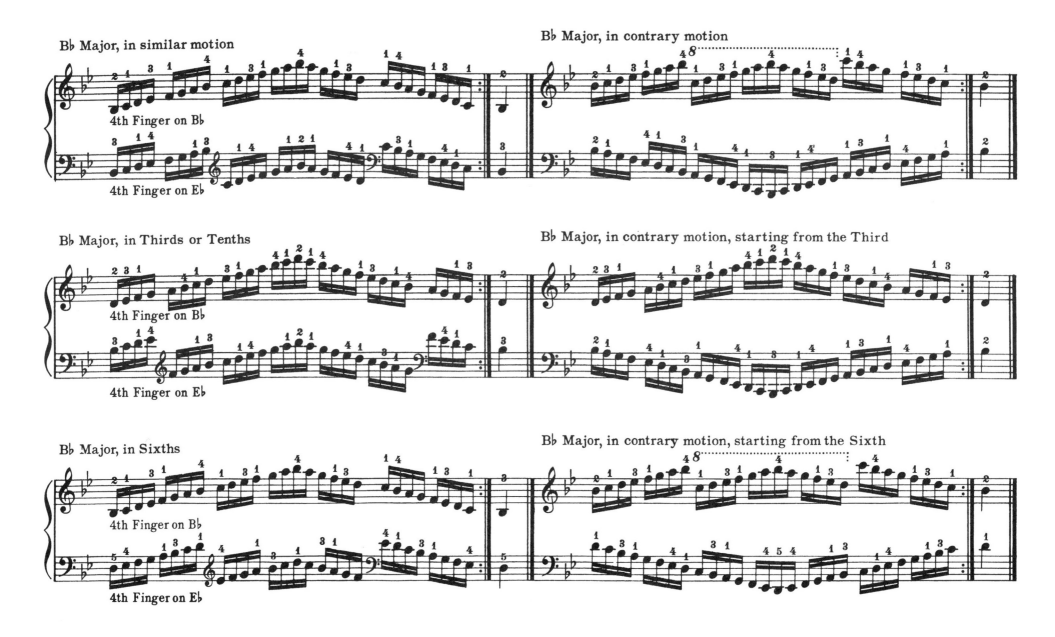

Bb Major, in similar motion

Bb Major, in contrary motion

4th Finger on Bb

4th Finger on Eb

Bb Major, in Thirds or Tenths

Bb Major, in contrary motion, starting from the Third

4th Finger on Bb

4th Finger on Eb

Bb Major, in Sixths

Bb Major, in contrary motion, starting from the Sixth

4th Finger on Bb

4th Finger on Eb

Harmonic Bb Minor, in similar motion

Harmonic Bb Minor, in contrary motion

4th Finger on Bb

4th Finger on Gb

Harmonic Bb Minor, in Thirds or Tenths

Harmonic Bb Minor, in contrary motion, starting from the Third

4th Finger on Bb

4th Finger on Gb

Harmonic Bb Minor, in Sixths

Harmonic Bb Minor, in contrary motion, starting from the Sixth

4th Finger on Bb

4th Finger on Gb

Arbitrary or Melodic Bb Minor, in similar motion

4th Finger on Bb

4th Finger on Gb ascending and Gb descending

Scale of F

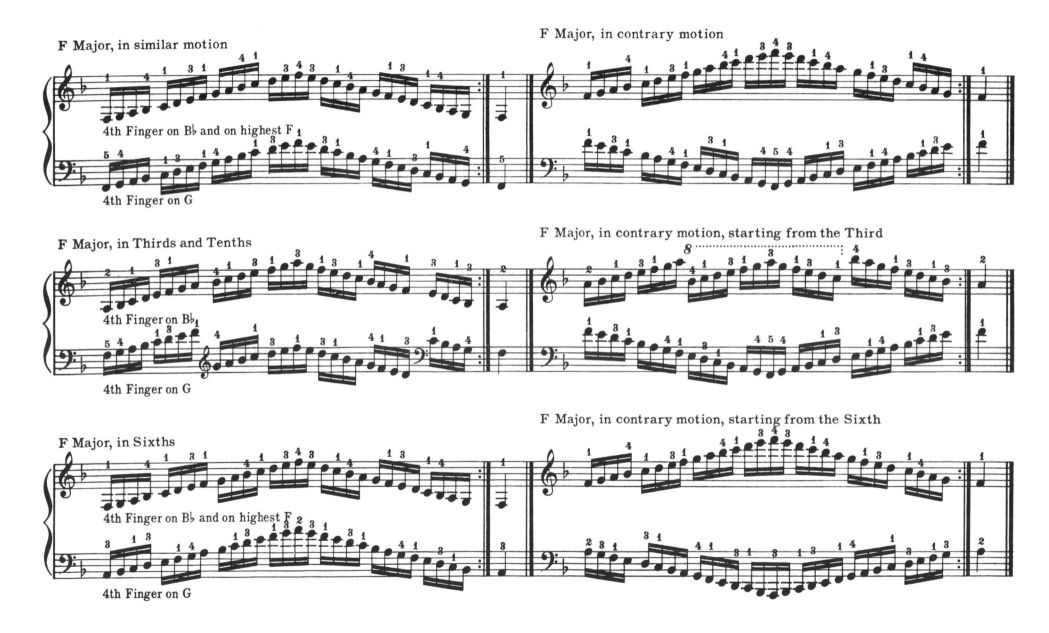

F Major, in similar motion

4th Finger on B♭ and on highest F

4th Finger on G

F Major, in contrary motion

F Major, in Thirds and Tenths

4th Finger on B♭

4th Finger on G

F Major, in contrary motion, starting from the Third

F Major, in Sixths

4th Finger on B♭ and on highest F

4th Finger on G

F Major, in contrary motion, starting from the Sixth

Harmonic F Minor, in similar motion

Harmonic F Minor, in contrary motion

4th Finger on B♭ and on highest F

4th Finger on G

Harmonic F Minor, in Thirds or Tenths

Harmonic F Minor, in contrary motion, starting from the Third

4th Finger on B♭

4th Finger on G

Harmonic F Minor, in Sixths

Harmonic F Minor, in contrary motion, starting from the Sixth

4th Finger on B♭ and on highest F

4th Finger on G

Arbitrary or Melodic F Minor, in similar motion

4th Finger on B♭ and on highest F

4th Finger on G

Chromatic Scale

In similar motion

3d Finger on all black keys

3d Finger on all black keys

In contrary motion

In Thirds, or Tenths

3d Finger on all black keys

3d Finger on all black keys

In contrary motion, starting from the Third

In Sixths

3d Finger on all black keys

3d Finger on all black keys

In contrary motion, starting from the Sixth

Another Method of Chromatic Scale Fingering

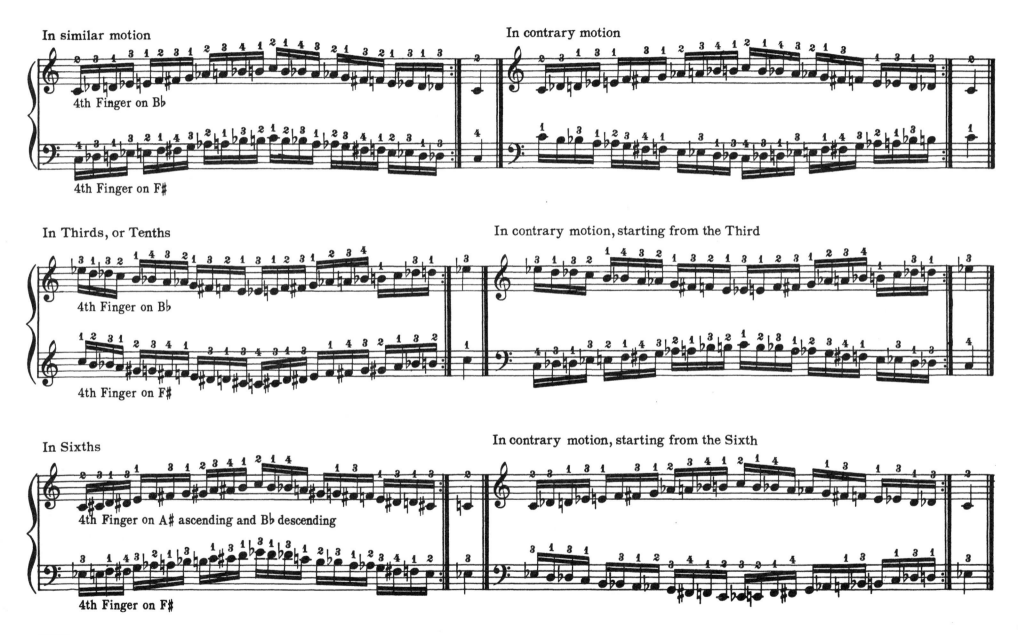

In similar motion

4th Finger on Bb

4th Finger on F#

In contrary motion

In Thirds, or Tenths

4th Finger on Bb

4th Finger on F#

In contrary motion, starting from the Third

In Sixths

4th Finger on A# ascending and Bb descending

4th Finger on F#

In contrary motion, starting from the Sixth

Arpeggios of Common Chords

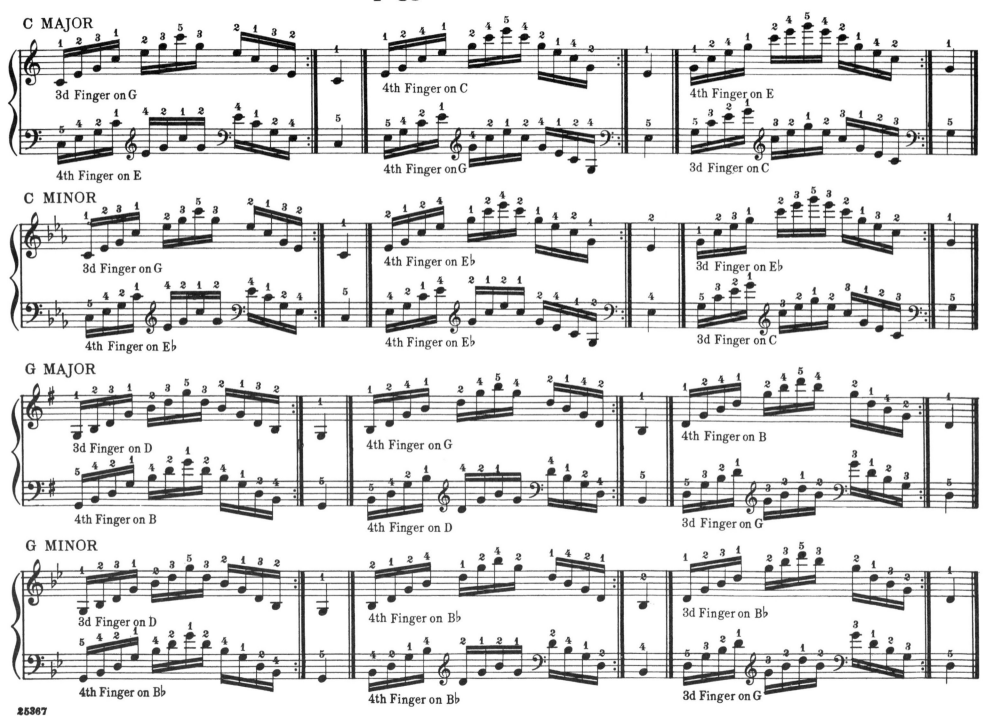

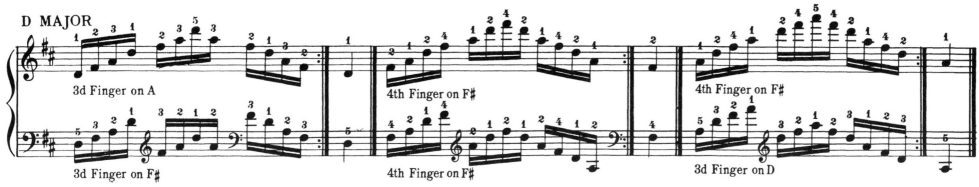

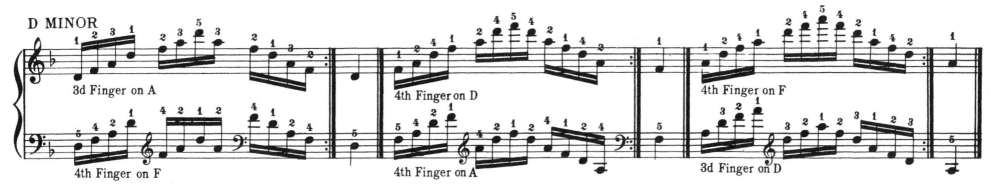

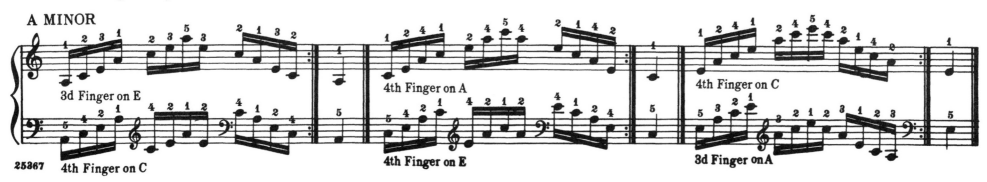

D MAJOR

3d Finger on A

3d Finger on F#

4th Finger on F#

4th Finger on F#

4th Finger on F#

3d Finger on D

D MINOR

3d Finger on A

4th Finger on D

4th Finger on F

4th Finger on F

4th Finger on A

3d Finger on D

A MAJOR

3d Finger on E

4th Finger on C#

4th Finger on C#

3d Finger on C#

4th Finger on C#

3d Finger on A

A MINOR

3d Finger on E

4th Finger on A

4th Finger on C

25867   4th Finger on C

4th Finger on E

3d Finger on A

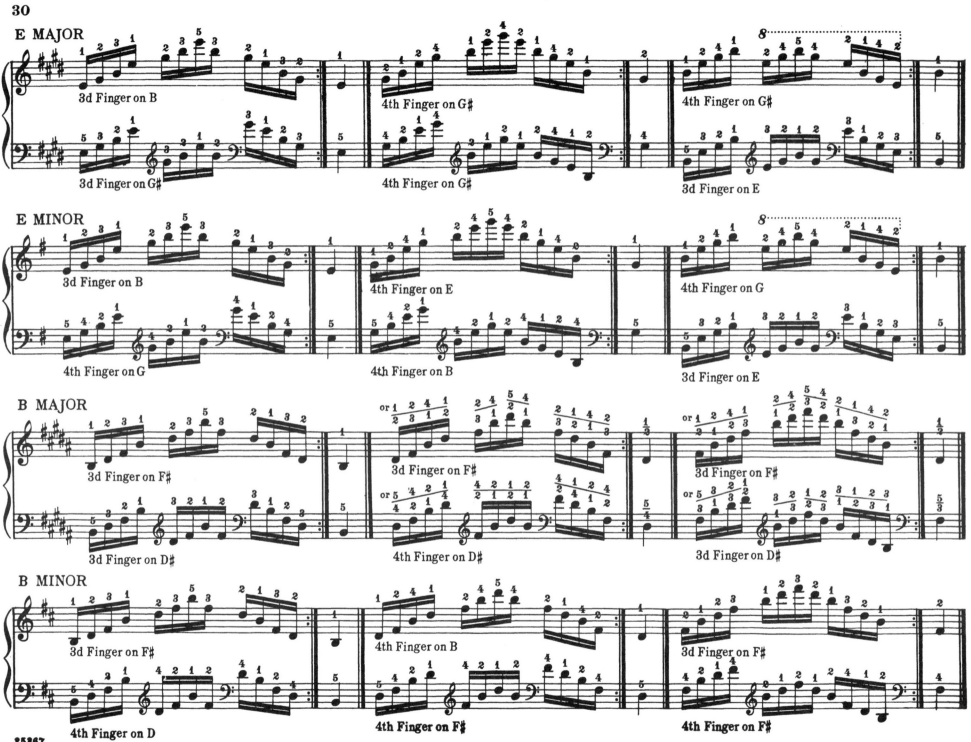

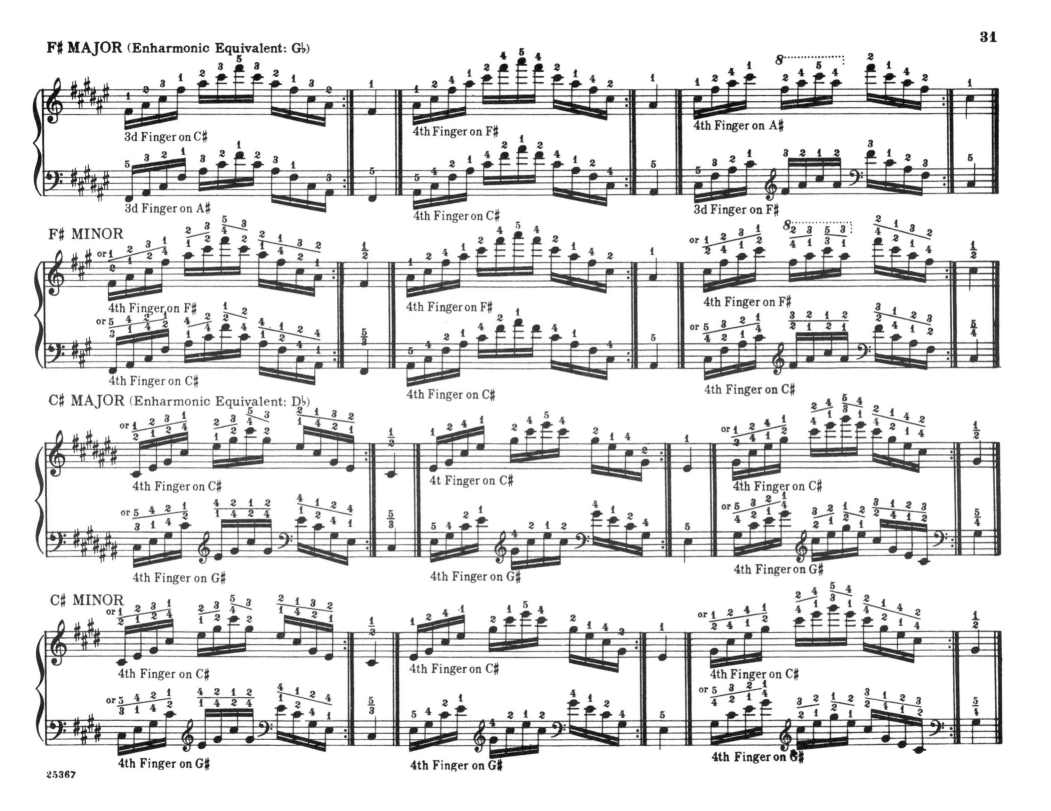

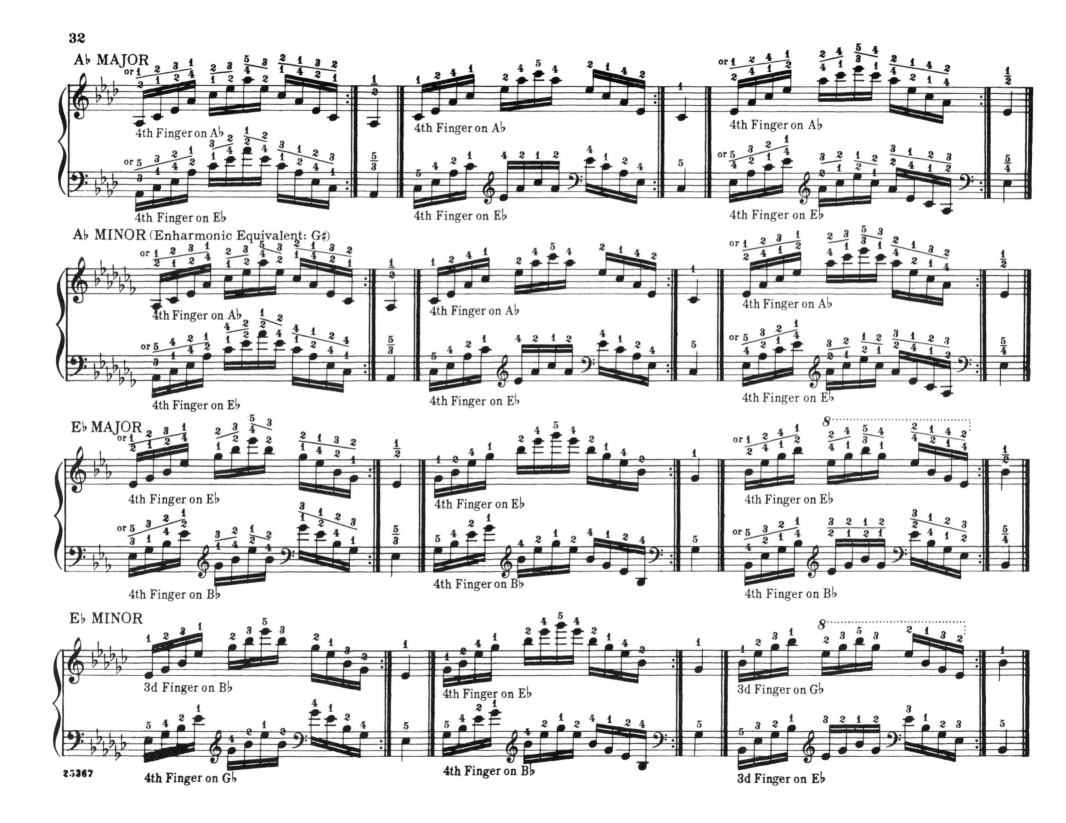

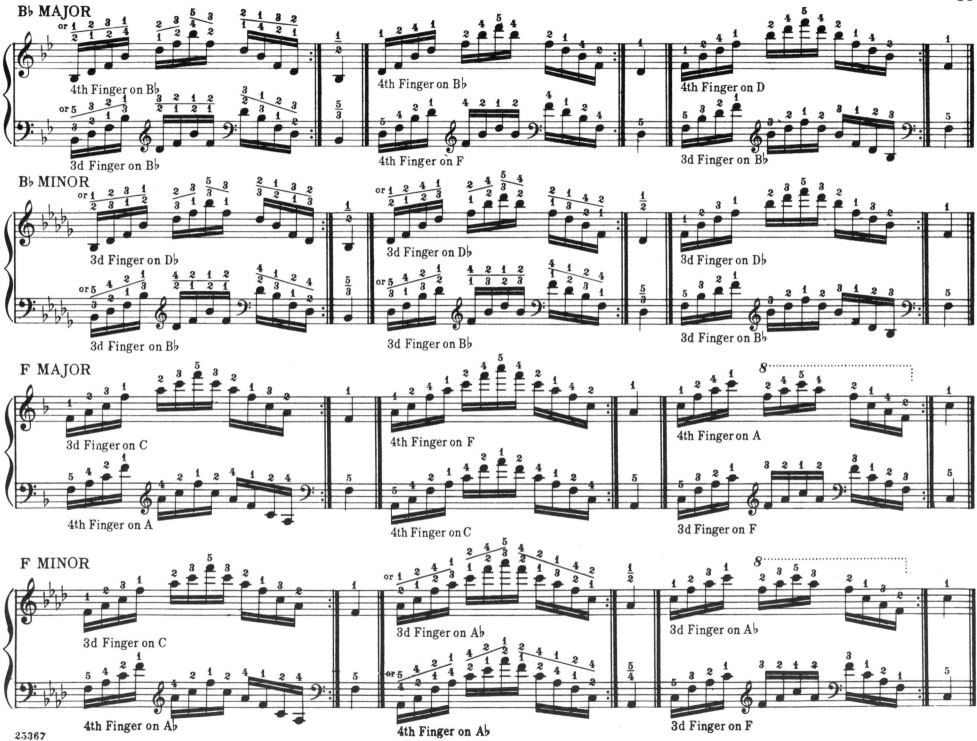

Arpeggios of Dominant Seventh-Chords

In the Key of C

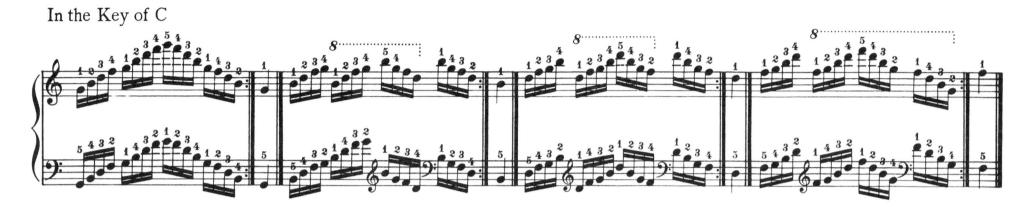

In the Key of G

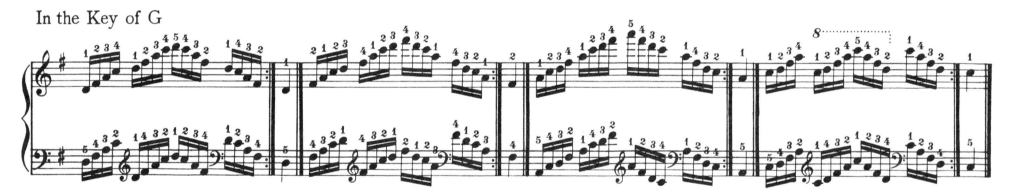

In the Key of D

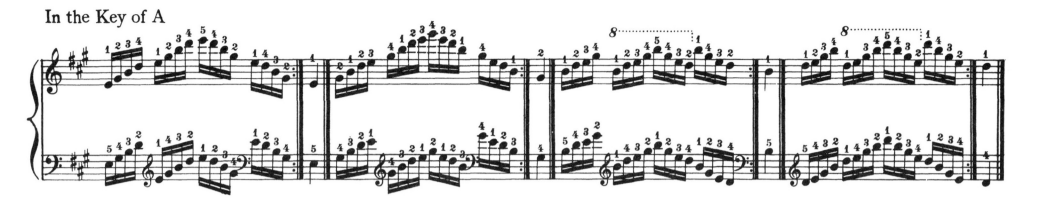

In the Key of A

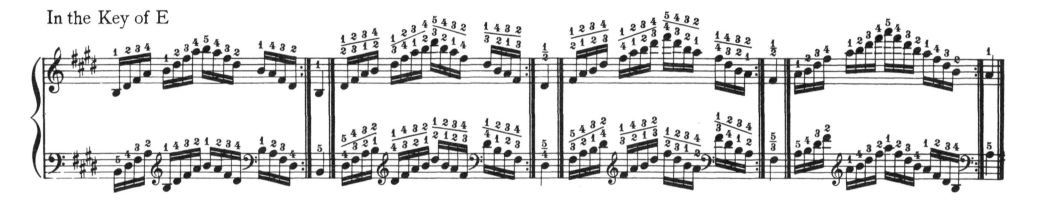

In the Key of E

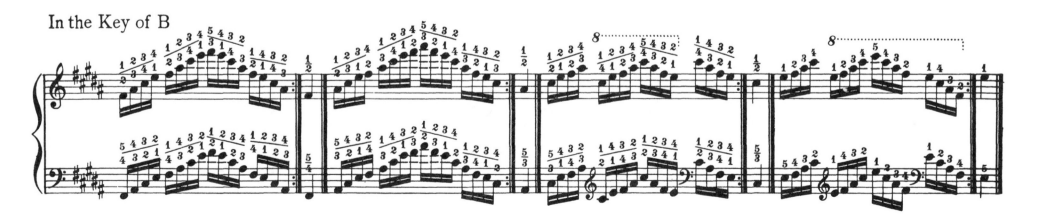

In the Key of B

In the Key of F♯ (Enharmonic Equivalent: G♭)

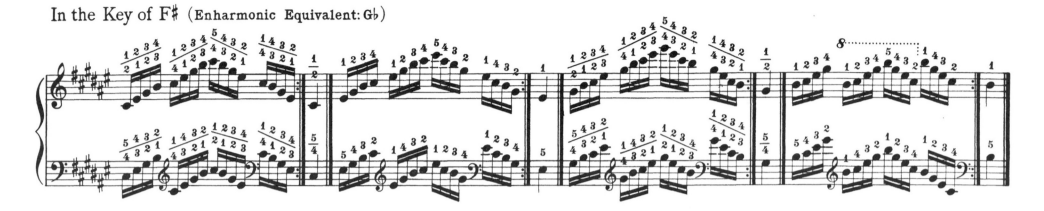

In the Key of C♯ (Enharmonic Equivalent: D♭)

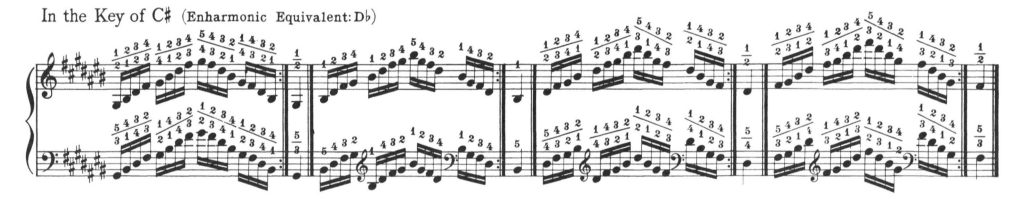

In the Key of A♭

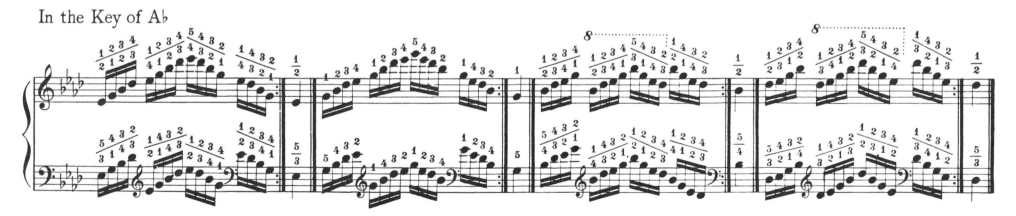

In the Key of E♭

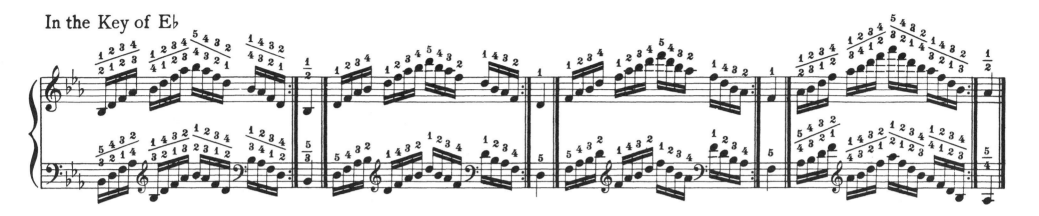

In the Key of B♭

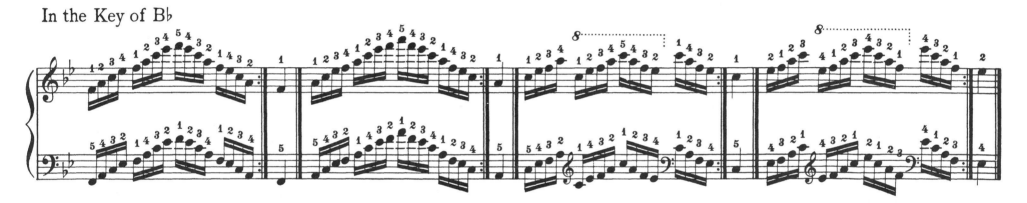

In the Key of F

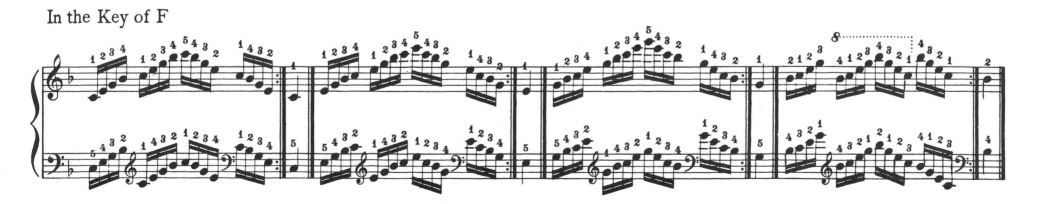

Arpeggios of Diminished Seventh-Chords

In the Key of C

In the Key of G

In the Key of D

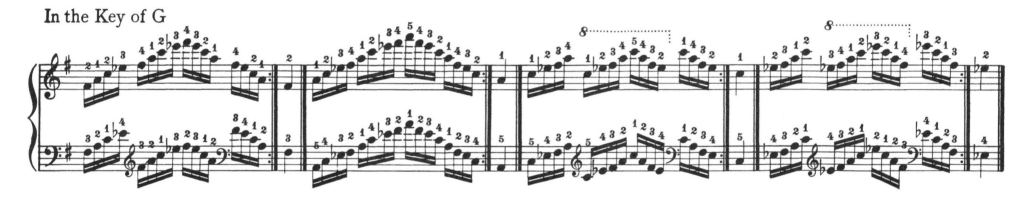

In the Key of A

In the Key of E

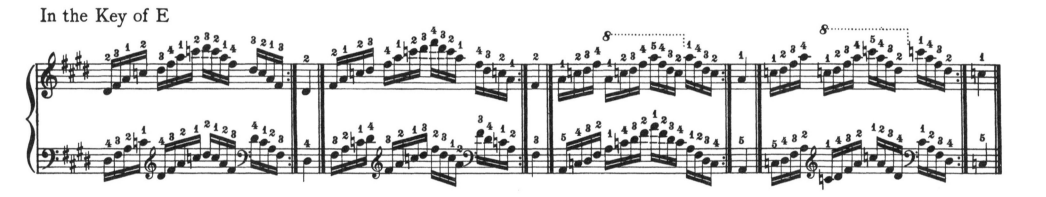

In the Key of B

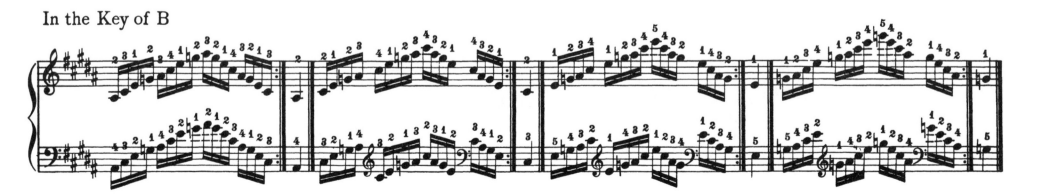

In the Key of F♯ (Enharmonic Equivalent: G♭)

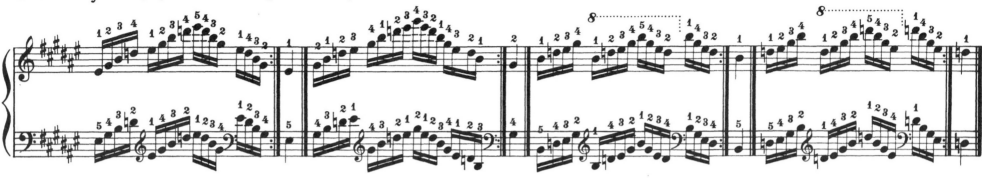

In the Key of C♯ (Enharmonic Equivalent: D♭)

In the Key of A♭

In the Key of E♭

In the Key of B♭

In the Key of F

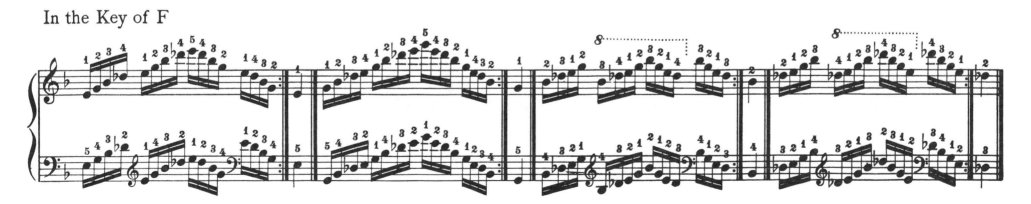

42

Scales in Double Thirds

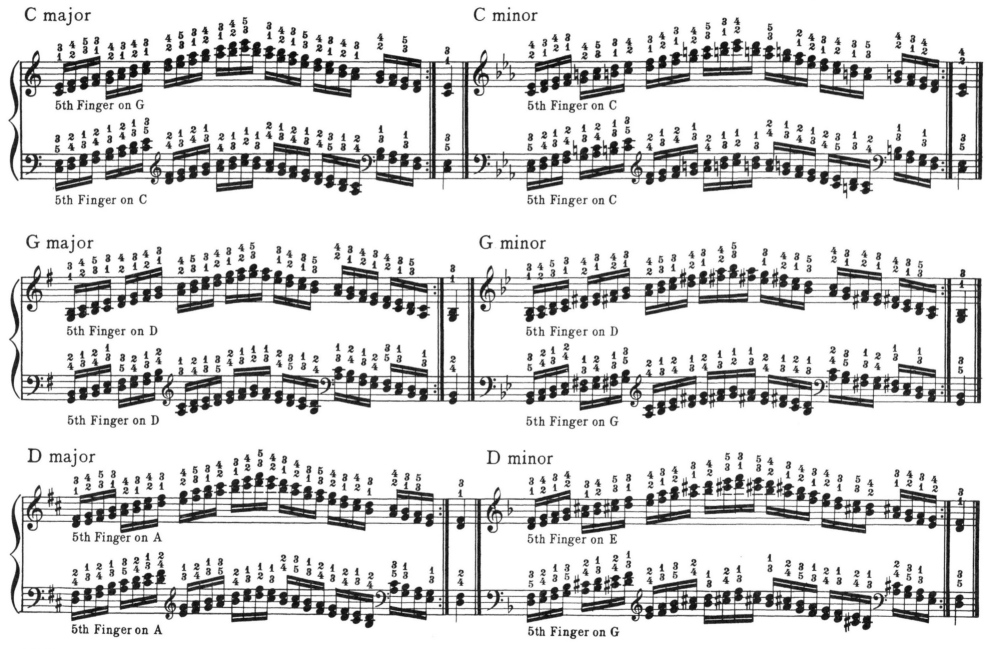

A major

A minor

5th Finger on E

5th Finger on B

5th Finger on A

5th Finger on E

E major

E minor

5th Finger on B

5th Finger on B

5th Finger on A

5th Finger on A

B major

B minor

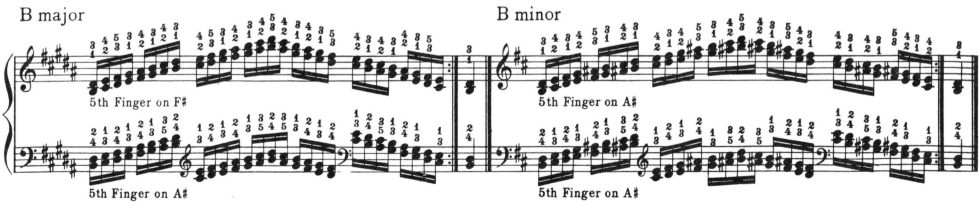

5th Finger on F#

5th Finger on A#

5th Finger on A#

5th Finger on A#

F# major

F# minor (Enharmonic Equivalent: G♭)

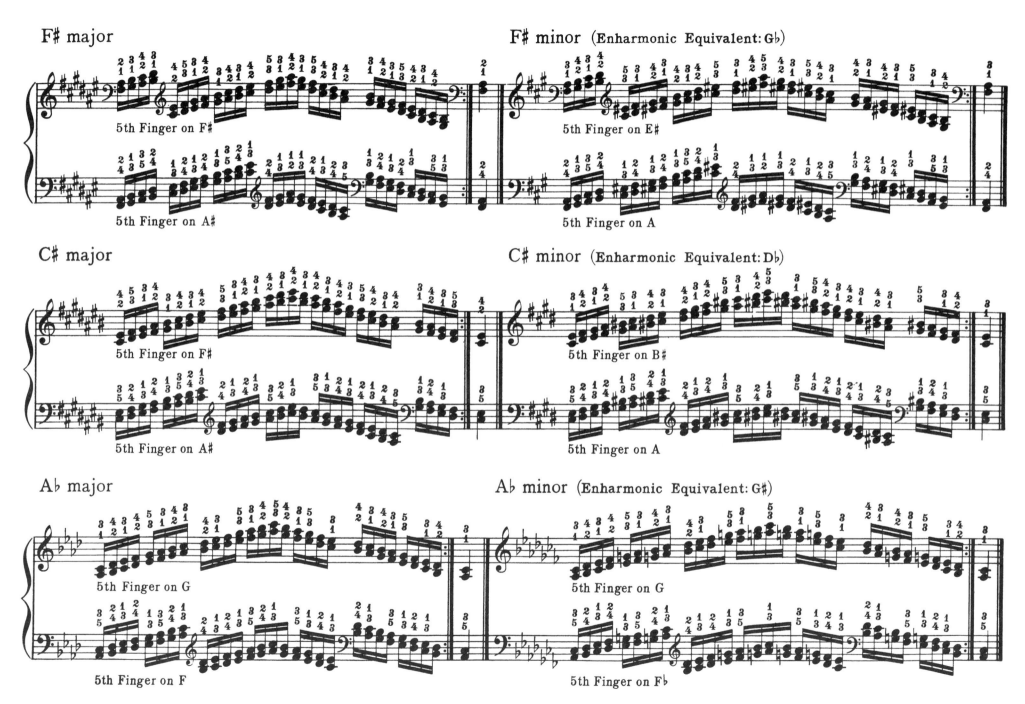

5th Finger on F#

5th Finger on E#

5th Finger on A#

5th Finger on A

C# major

C# minor (Enharmonic Equivalent: D♭)

5th Finger on F#

5th Finger on B#

5th Finger on A#

5th Finger on A

A♭ major

A♭ minor (Enharmonic Equivalent: G♯)

5th Finger on G

5th Finger on G

5th Finger on F

5th Finger on F♭

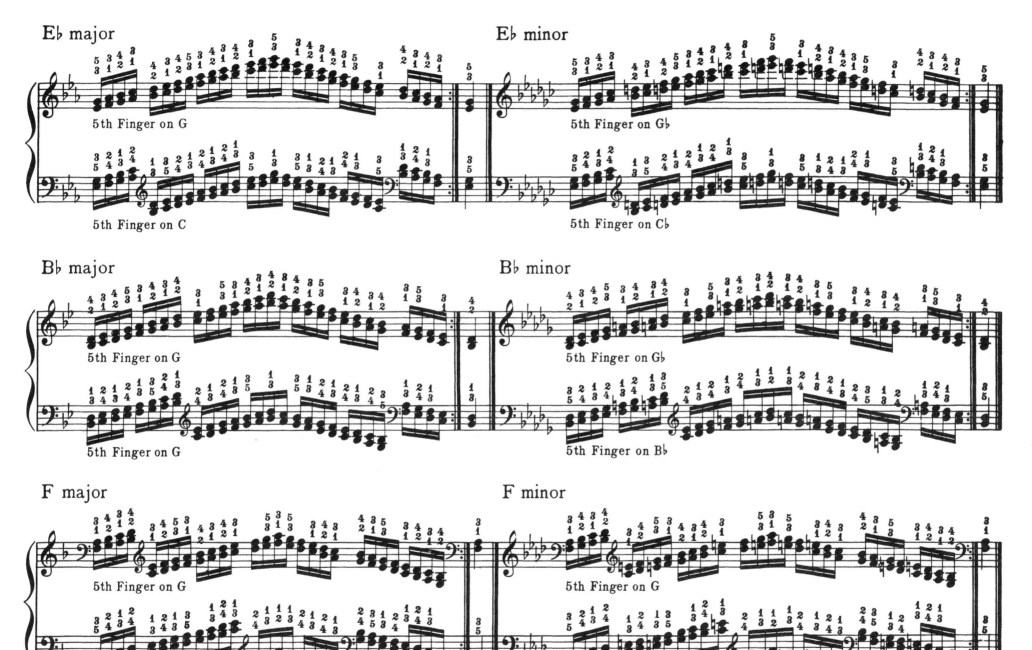

Eb major — 5th Finger on G / 5th Finger on C

Eb minor — 5th Finger on Gb / 5th Finger on Cb

Bb major — 5th Finger on G / 5th Finger on G

Bb minor — 5th Finger on Gb / 5th Finger on Bb

F major — 5th Finger on G / 5th Finger on F

F minor — 5th Finger on G / 5th Finger on F

Scales in Double Sixths

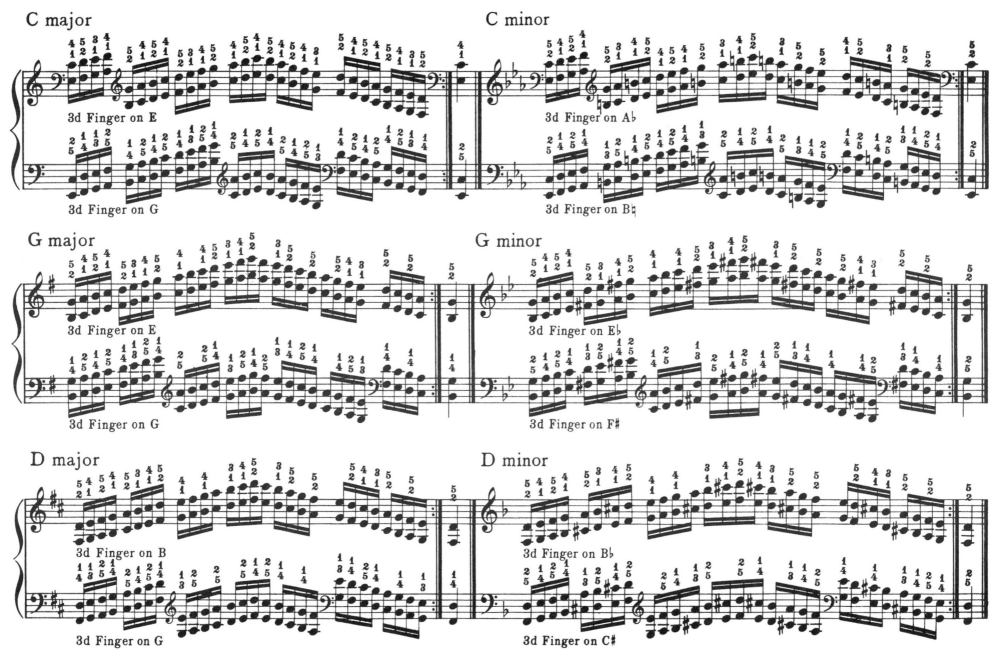

C major

3d Finger on E

3d Finger on G

C minor

3d Finger on A♭

3d Finger on B♮

G major

3d Finger on E

3d Finger on G

G minor

3d Finger on E♭

3d Finger on F♯

D major

3d Finger on B

3d Finger on G

D minor

3d Finger on B♭

3d Finger on C♯

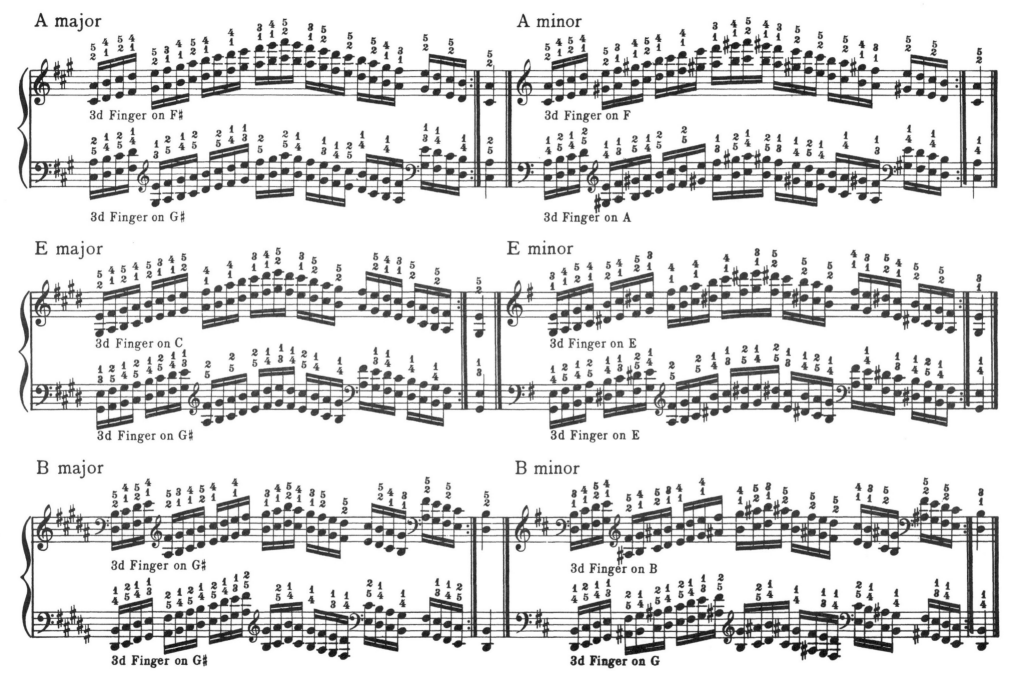

F♯ major

F♯ minor (Enharmonic Equivalent: G♭)

3d Finger on G♯

3d Finger on F♯

3d Finger on G♯

3d Finger on G♯

C♯ major

C♯ minor (Enharmonic Equivalent: D♭)

3d Finger on G♯

3d Finger on C♯

3d Finger on G♯

3d Finger on G♯

A♭ major

A♭ minor

3d Finger on A♭

3d Finger on A♭

3d Finger on E♭

3d Finger on E♭

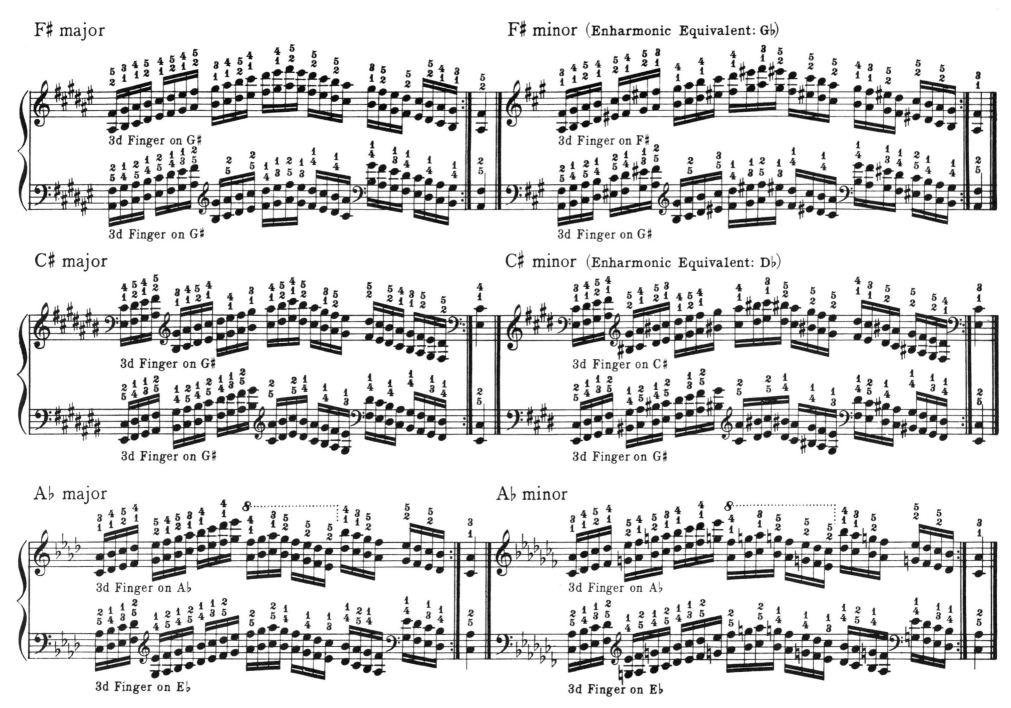

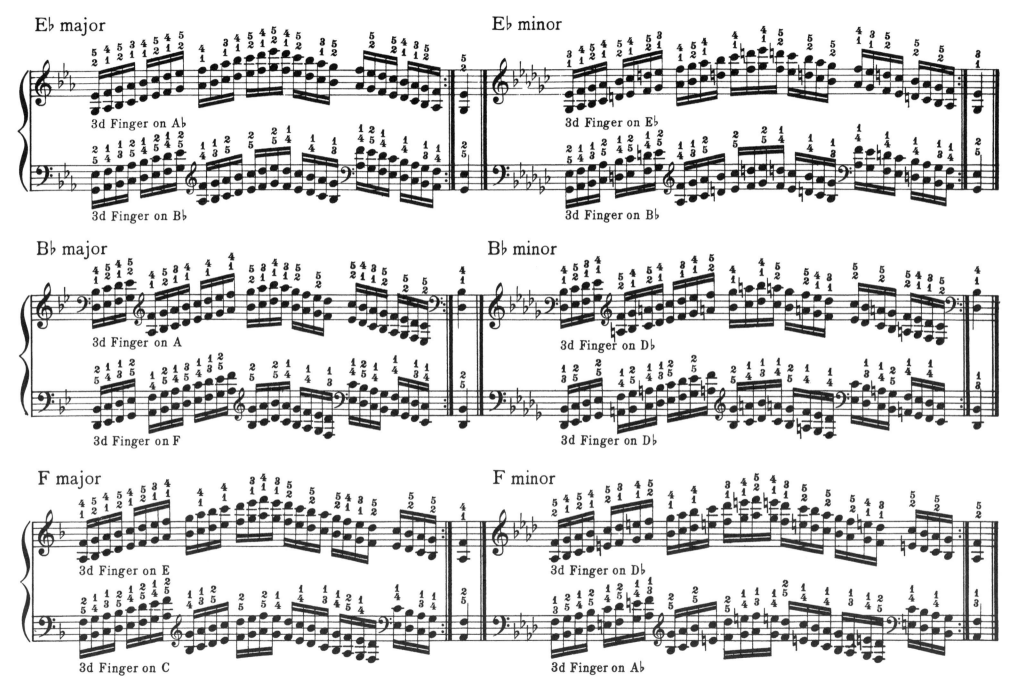

Chromatic Scale in Double Minor Thirds

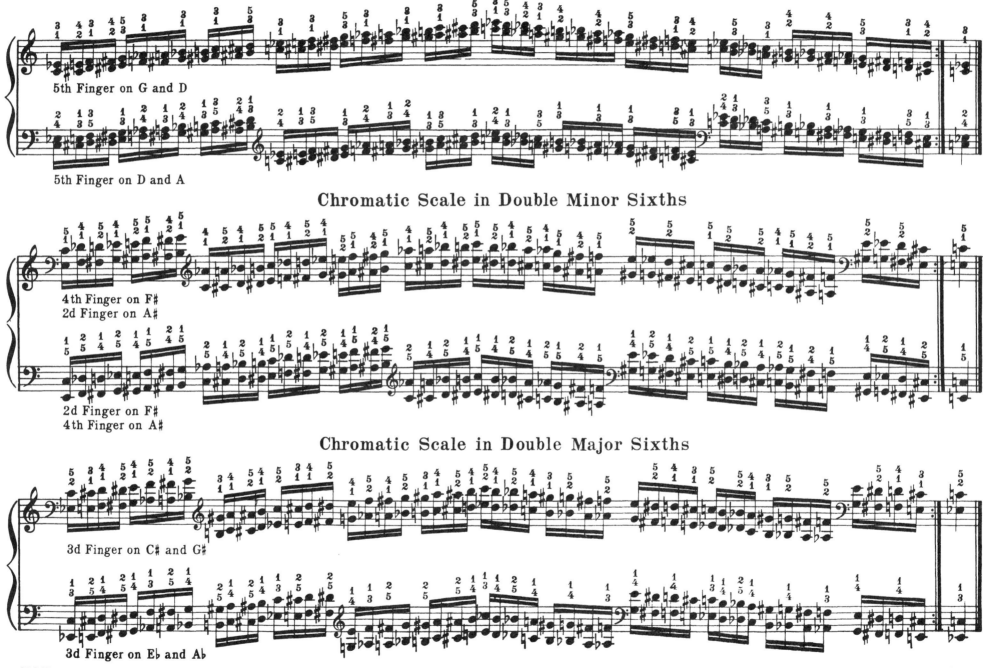

5th Finger on G and D

5th Finger on D and A

Chromatic Scale in Double Minor Sixths

4th Finger on F♯
2d Finger on A♯

2d Finger on F♯
4th Finger on A♯

Chromatic Scale in Double Major Sixths

3d Finger on C♯ and G♯

3d Finger on E♭ and A♭

Chromatic Scale in Complete Chords of the Sixth

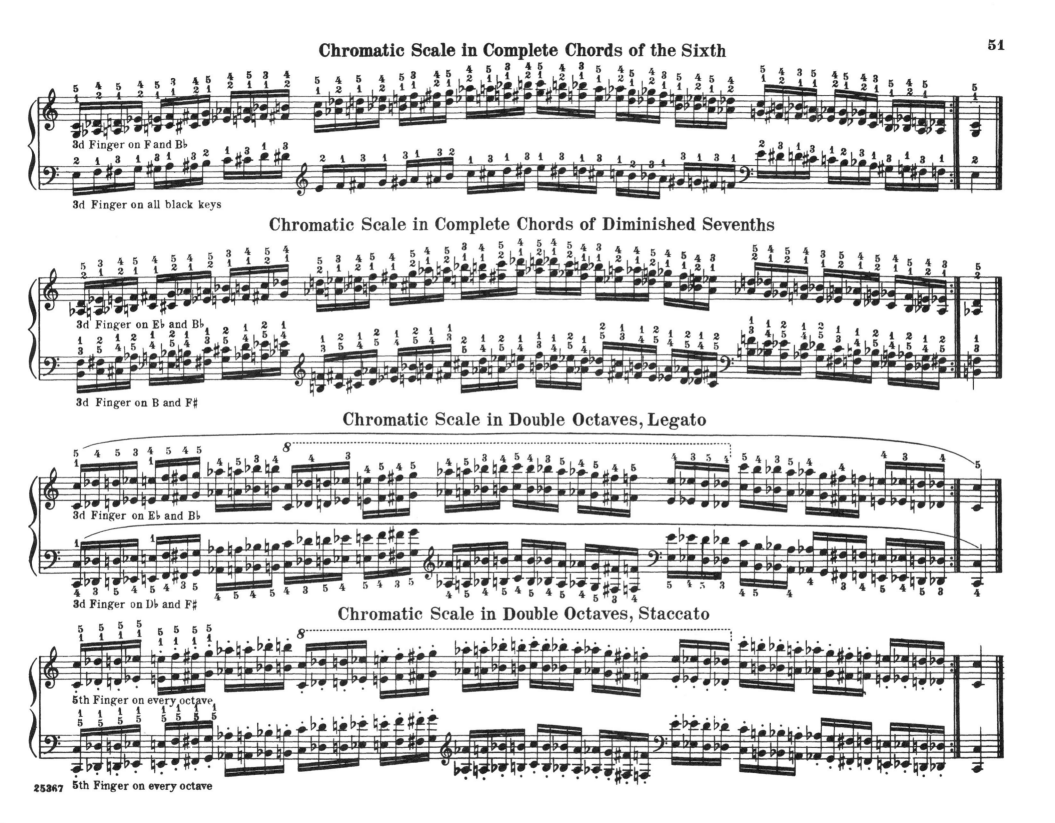

3d Finger on F and B♭

3d Finger on all black keys

Chromatic Scale in Complete Chords of Diminished Sevenths

3d Finger on E♭ and B♭

3d Finger on B and F♯

Chromatic Scale in Double Octaves, Legato

3d Finger on E♭ and B♭

3d Finger on D♭ and F♯

Chromatic Scale in Double Octaves, Staccato

5th Finger on every octave

5th Finger on every octave

Scales in Double Octaves

C major, legato

5th Finger on every octave

5th Finger on every octave

C minor, legato

4th Finger on all black keys

4th Finger on all black keys

C major, staccato

5th Finger on every octave

5th Finger on every octave

C minor, staccato

5th Finger on every octave

5th Finger on every octave

G major, legato

4th Finger on all black keys

4th Finger on all black keys

G minor, legato

4th Finger on all black keys

4th Finger on all black keys

G major, staccato

D major, legato

D major, staccato

G minor, staccato

D minor, legato

D minor, staccato

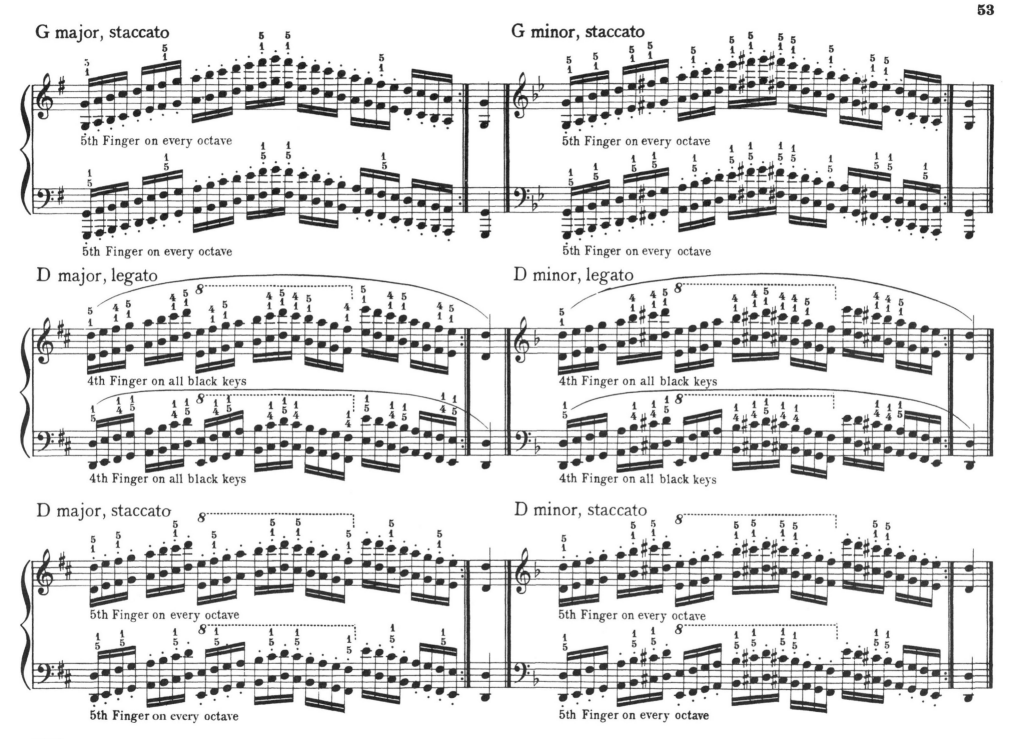

5th Finger on every octave

5th Finger on every octave

4th Finger on all black keys

4th Finger on all black keys

5th Finger on every octave

5th Finger on every octave

5th Finger on every octave

5th Finger on every octave

4th Finger on all black keys

4th Finger on all black keys

5th Finger on every octave

5th Finger on every octave

A major, legato

A minor, legato

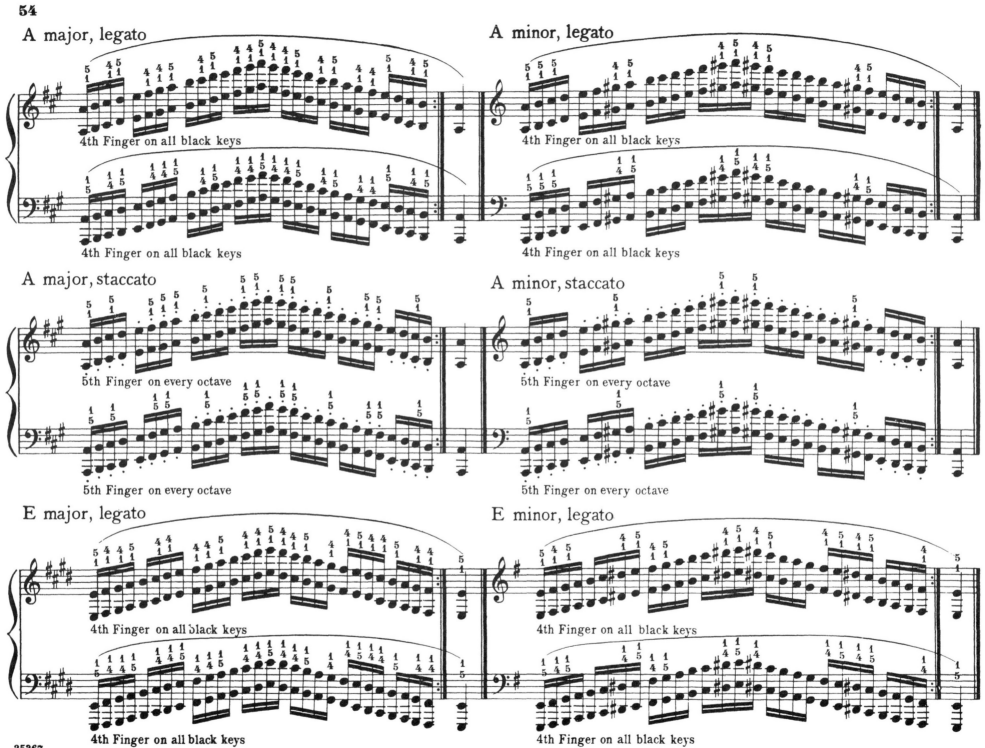

4th Finger on all black keys

4th Finger on all black keys

4th Finger on all black keys

4th Finger on all black keys

A major, staccato

A minor, staccato

5th Finger on every octave

5th Finger on every octave

5th Finger on every octave

5th Finger on every octave

E major, legato

E minor, legato

4th Finger on all black keys

4th Finger on all black keys

4th Finger on all black keys

4th Finger on all black keys

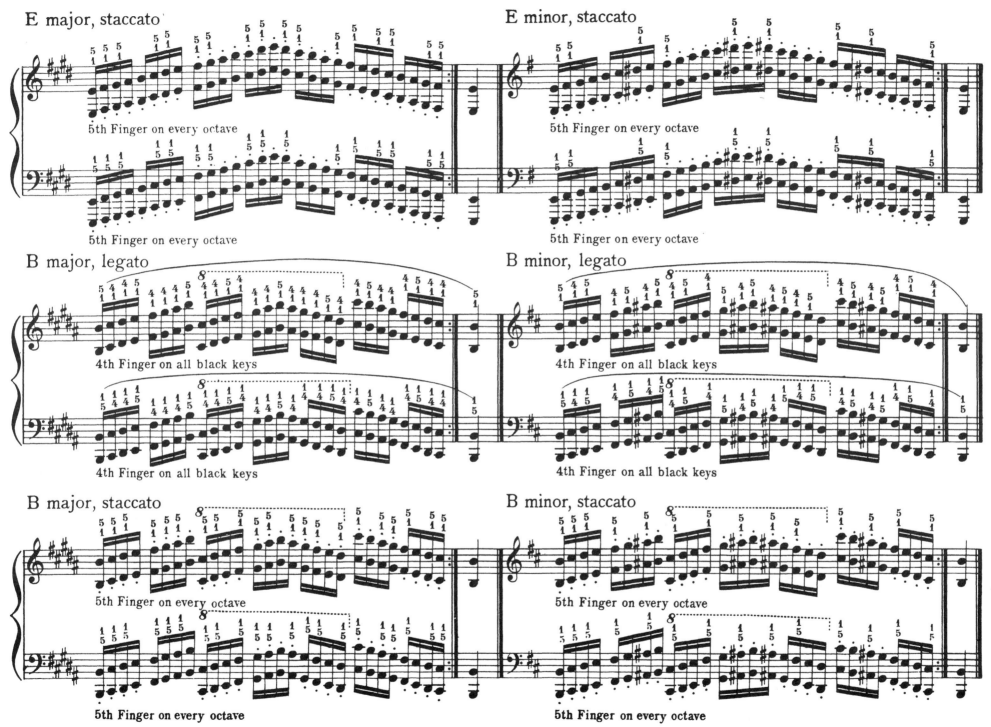

56

F# major (Enharm. Equiv.: Gb), legato

F# minor (Enharm. Equiv.: Gb), legato

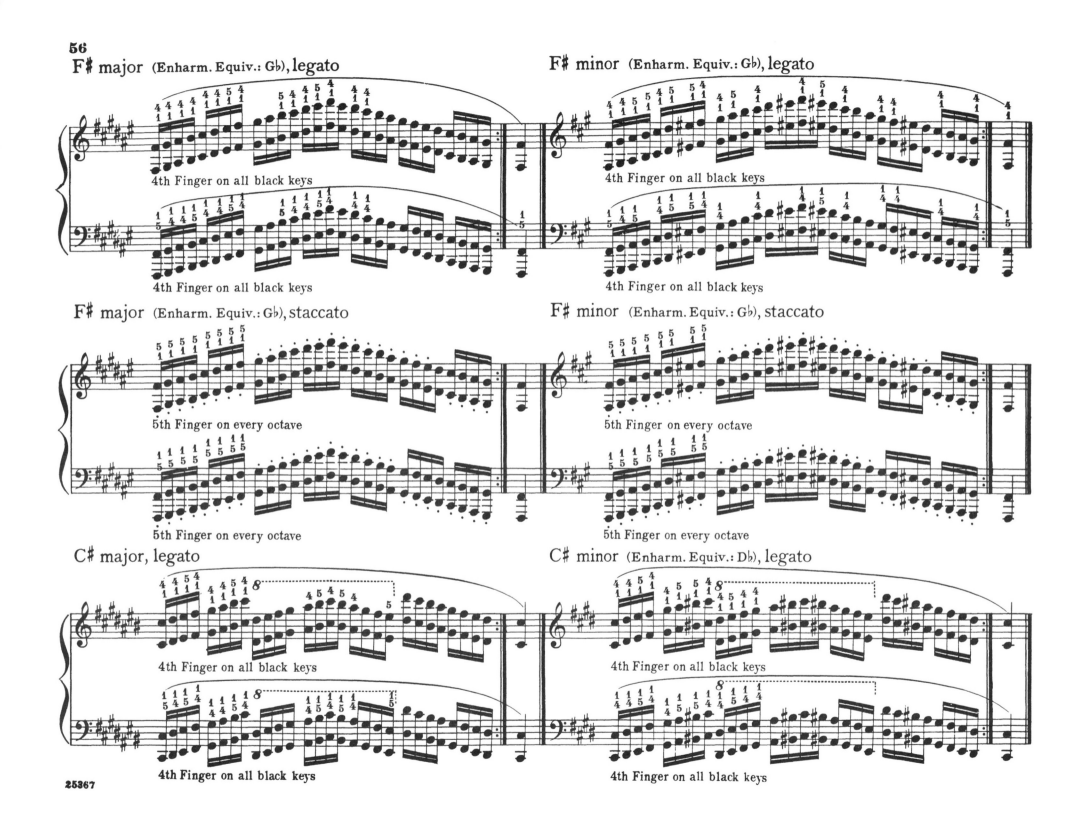

F# major (Enharm. Equiv.: Gb), staccato

F# minor (Enharm. Equiv.: Gb), staccato

C# major, legato

C# minor (Enharm. Equiv.: Db), legato

25367

C# major, staccato

C# minor (Enharm. Equiv.: Db), staccato

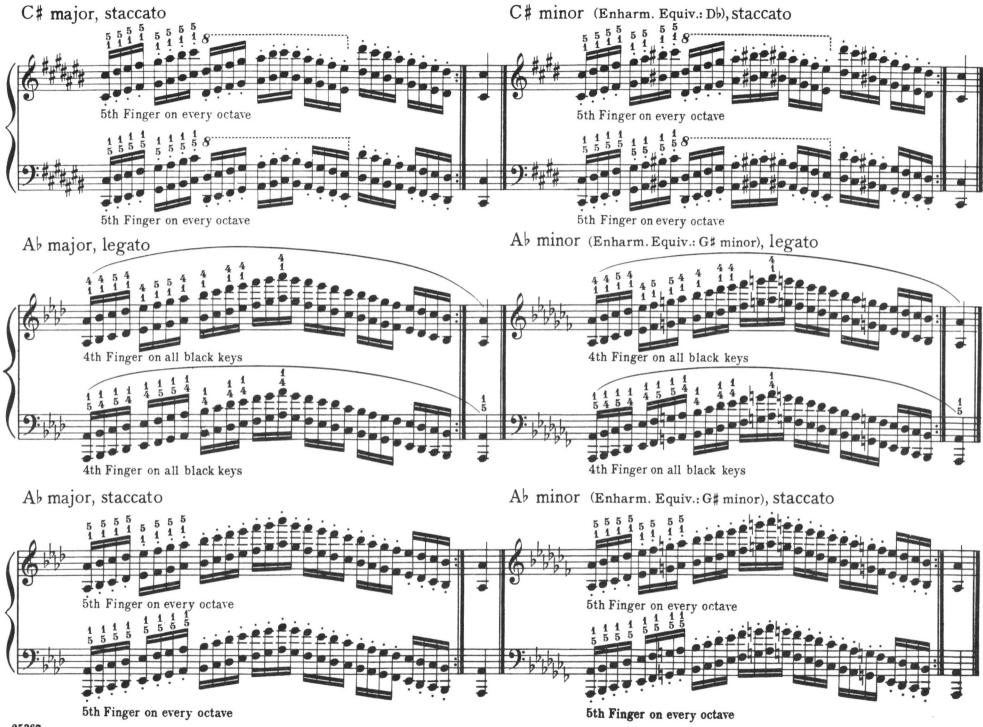

5th Finger on every octave

5th Finger on every octave

5th Finger on every octave

5th Finger on every octave

Ab major, legato

Ab minor (Enharm. Equiv.: G# minor), legato

4th Finger on all black keys

4th Finger on all black keys

4th Finger on all black keys

4th Finger on all black keys

Ab major, staccato

Ab minor (Enharm. Equiv.: G# minor), staccato

5th Finger on every octave

5th Finger on every octave

5th Finger on every octave

5th Finger on every octave

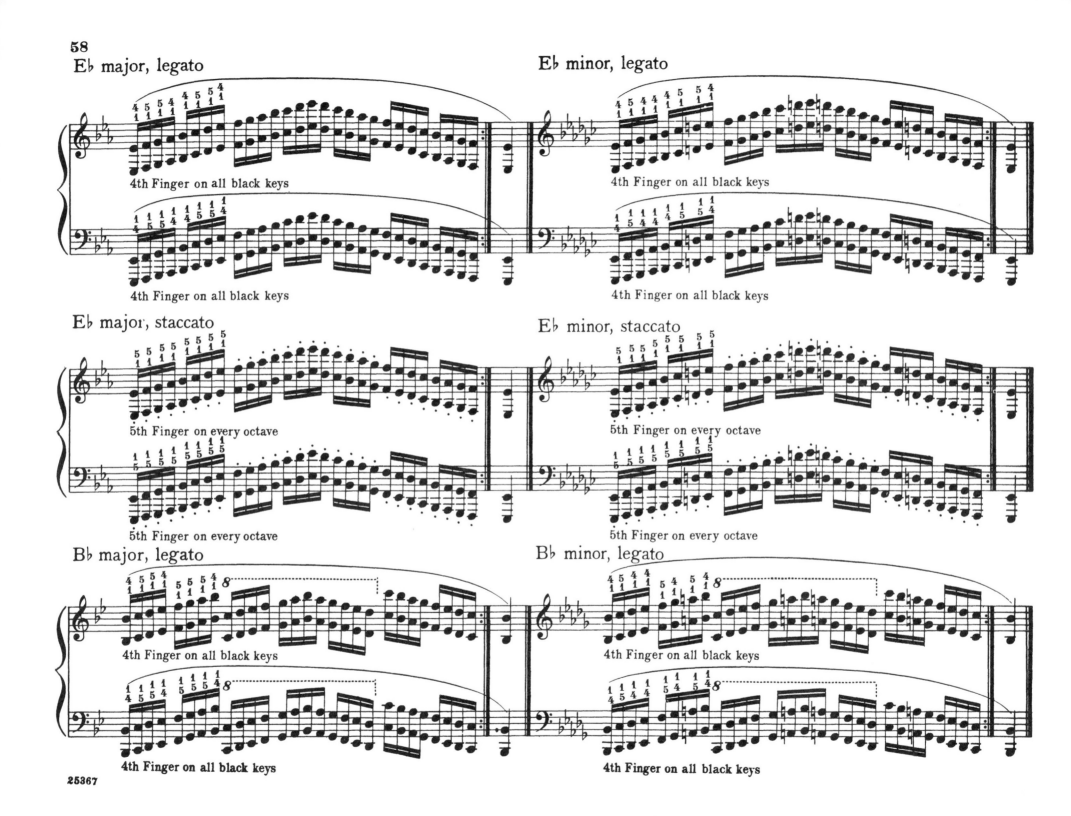

Eb major, legato

4th Finger on all black keys

4th Finger on all black keys

Eb minor, legato

4th Finger on all black keys

4th Finger on all black keys

Eb major, staccato

5th Finger on every octave

5th Finger on every octave

Eb minor, staccato

5th Finger on every octave

5th Finger on every octave

Bb major, legato

4th Finger on all black keys

4th Finger on all black keys

Bb minor, legato

4th Finger on all black keys

4th Finger on all black keys

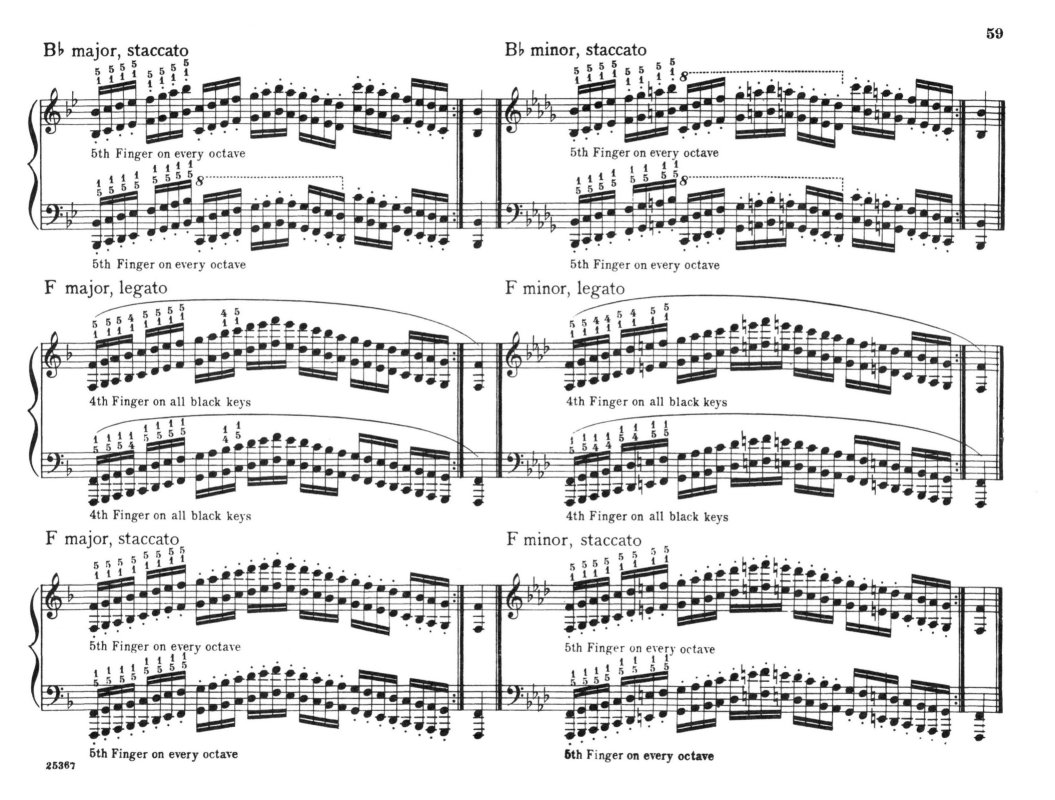

Bb major, staccato

5th Finger on every octave

5th Finger on every octave

Bb minor, staccato

5th Finger on every octave

5th Finger on every octave

F major, legato

4th Finger on all black keys

4th Finger on all black keys

F minor, legato

4th Finger on all black keys

4th Finger on all black keys

F major, staccato

5th Finger on every octave

5th Finger on every octave

F minor, staccato

5th Finger on every octave

5th Finger on every octave

Appendix

Scale of C

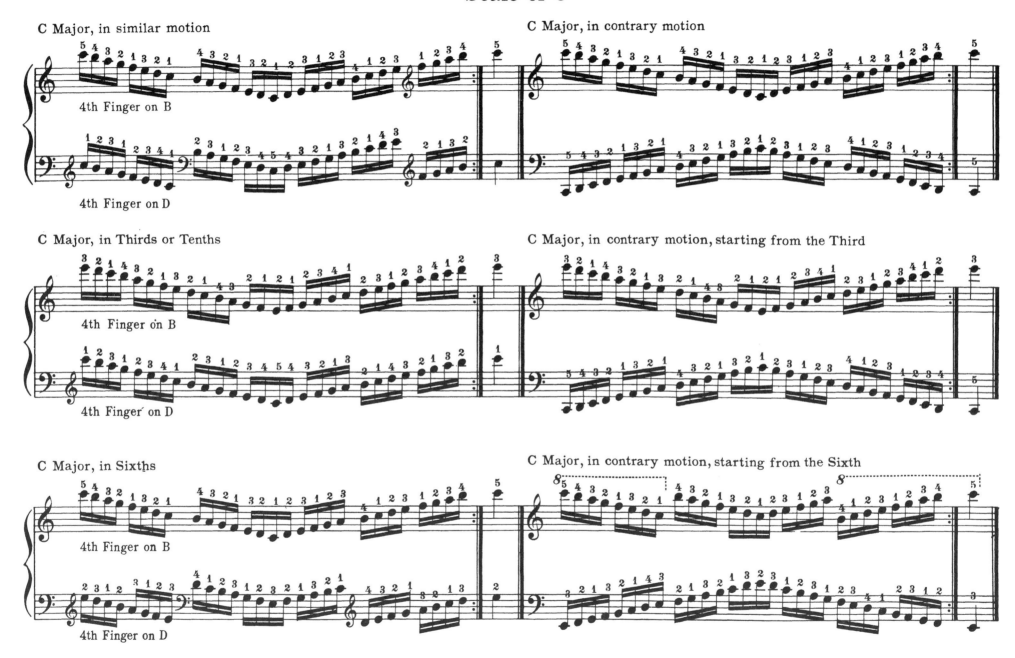

Harmonic C Minor, in similar motion

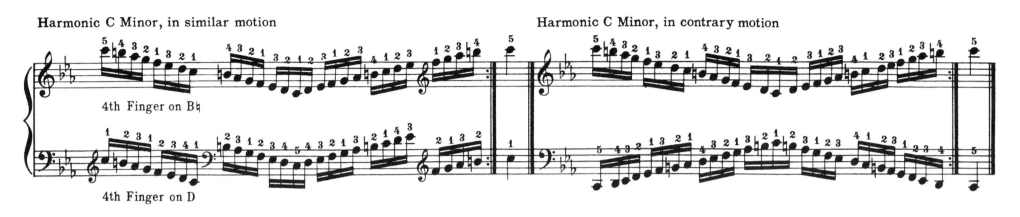

4th Finger on B♮

4th Finger on D

Harmonic C Minor, in contrary motion

Harmonic C Minor, in Thirds or Tenths

4th Finger on B♮

4th Finger on D

Harmonic C Minor, in contrary motion, starting from the Third

Harmonic C Minor, in Sixths

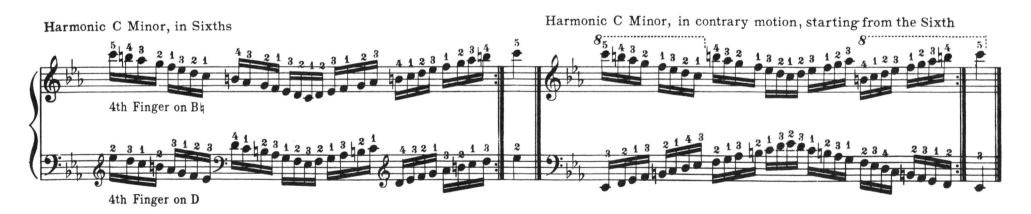

4th Finger on B♮

4th Finger on D

Harmonic C Minor, in contrary motion, starting from the Sixth

25367

Double Thirds, C Major and Minor, in similar motion

Double Thirds, C Major, in contrary motion

Double Thirds, C Minor, in contrary motion

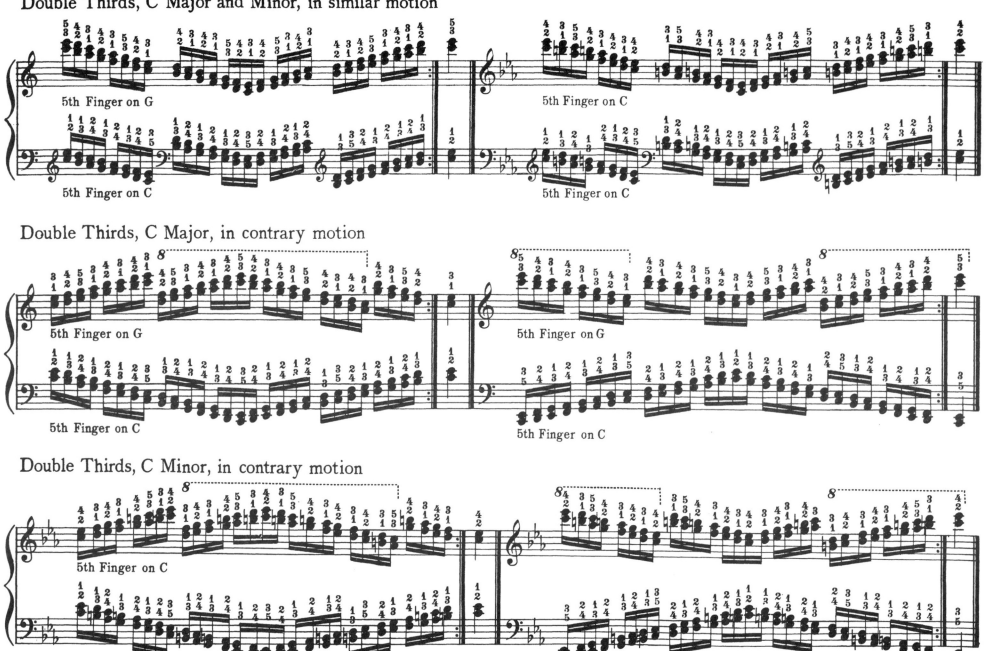

Double Sixths, C Major and Minor, in similar motion

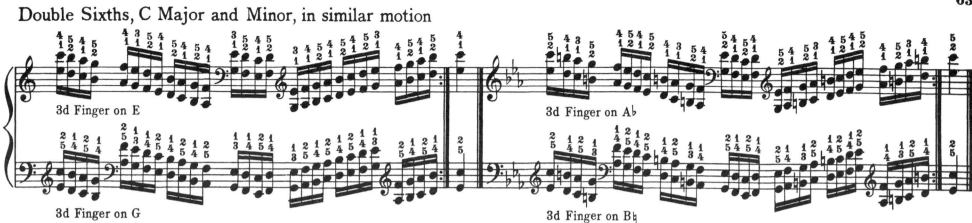

Double Sixths, C Major, in contrary motion

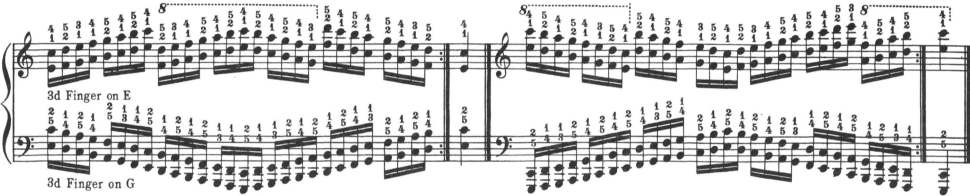

Double Sixths, C Minor, in contrary motion

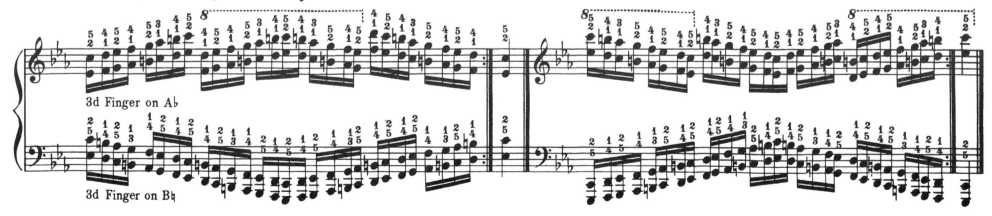

Double Octaves, C Major and Minor, in similar motion

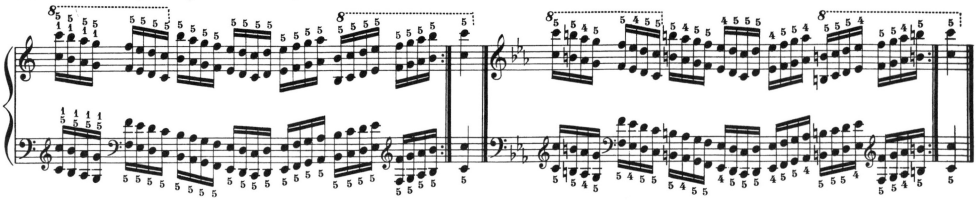

Double Octaves, C Major, in contrary motion

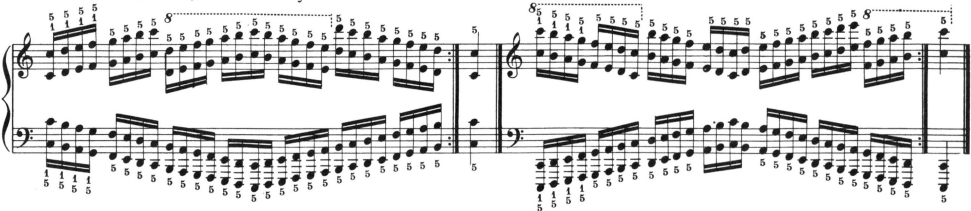

Double Octaves, C Minor, in contrary motion

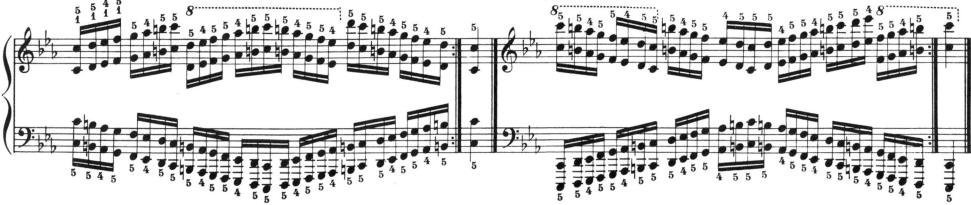

Double Octaves, C Major, in Thirds

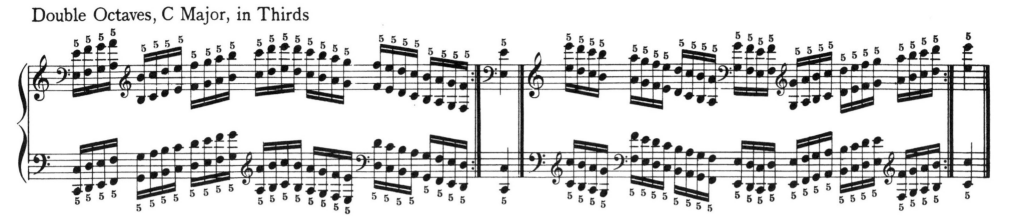

Double Octaves, C Major, in contrary motion, starting from the Third

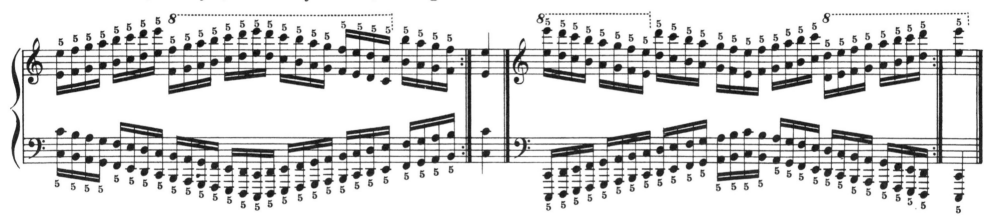

Double Octaves, C Major, in Sixths

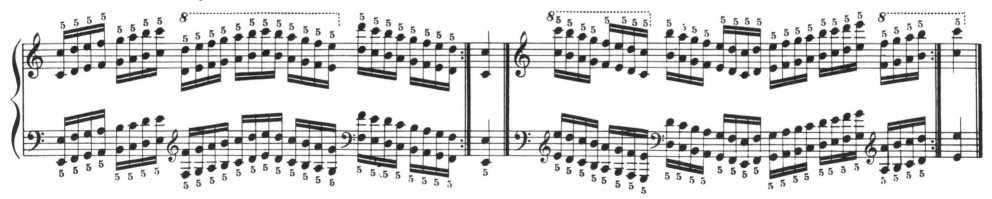

Double Octaves, C Major, in contrary motion, starting from the Sixth

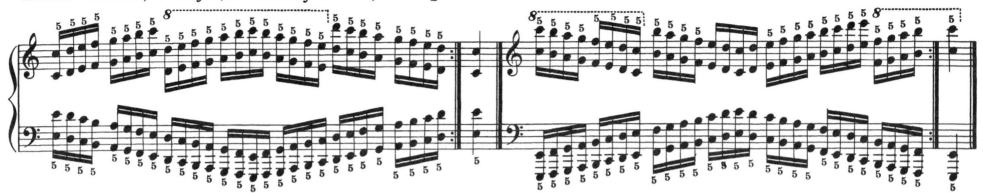

Double Octaves, C Minor, in Thirds

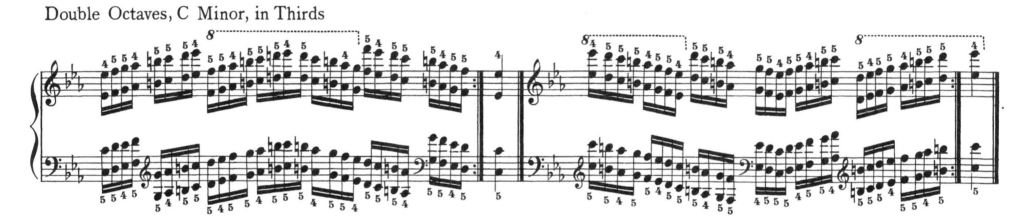

Double Octaves, C Minor, in contrary motion, starting from the Third

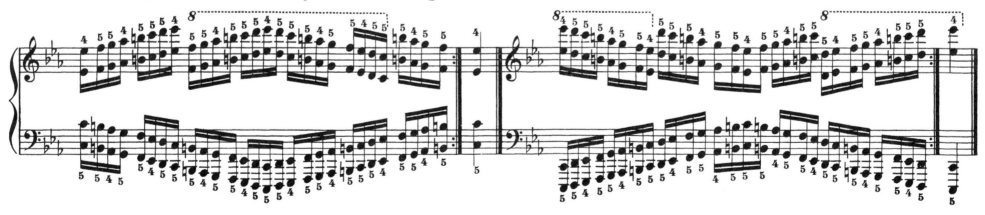

Double Octaves, C Minor, in Sixths

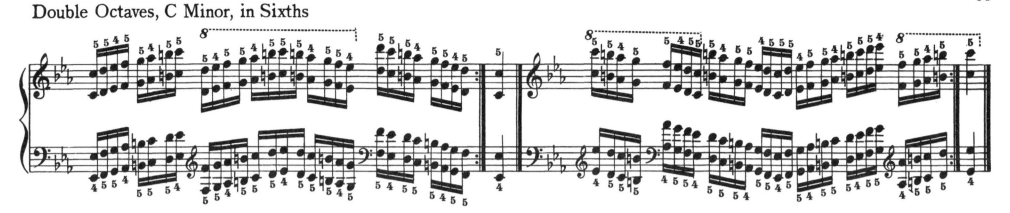

Double Octaves, C Minor, in contrary motion, starting from the Sixth

Chromatic Scale in Double Octaves

When played staccato, 5th Finger on every octave

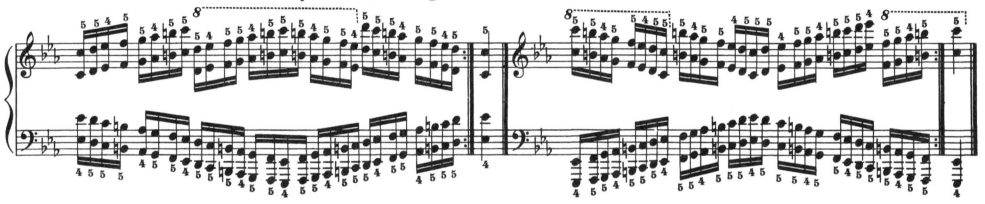

3d Finger on E♭ and B♭

3d Finger on D♭ and F♯

Double Octaves, in contrary motion

3d Finger on E♭ and B♭

3d Finger on D♭ and F♯

Double Octaves, in Thirds

3d Finger on E♭ and B♭

3d Finger on D♭ and F♯

Double Octaves, in contrary motion, starting from the Third

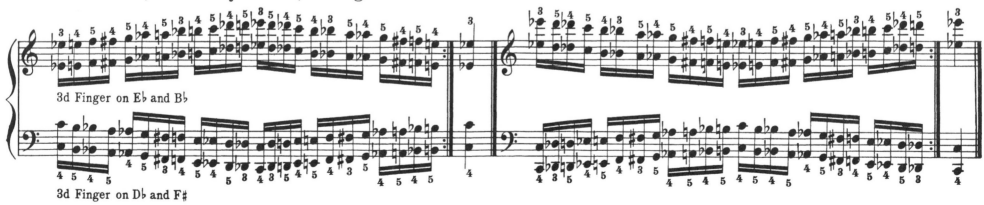

3d Finger on E♭ and B♭

3d Finger on D♭ and F♯

Double Octaves, in Minor Sixths, in similar and contrary motion

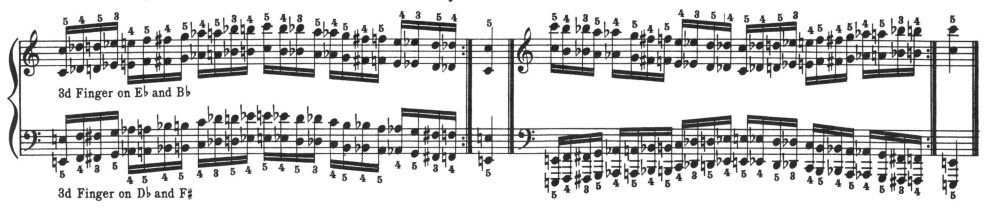

3d Finger on E♭ and B♭

3d Finger on D♭ and F♯

Double Octaves, in Major Sixths

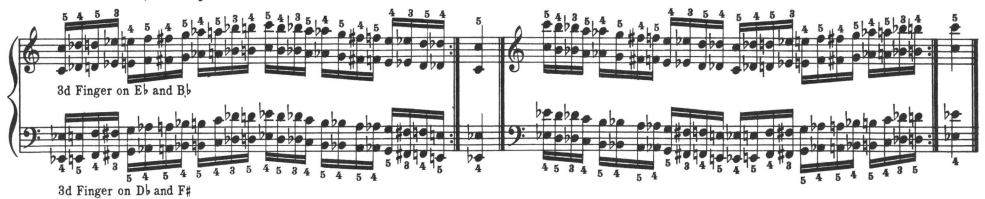

3d Finger on E♭ and B♭

3d Finger on D♭ and F♯

Double Octaves, in contrary motion, starting from the Sixth

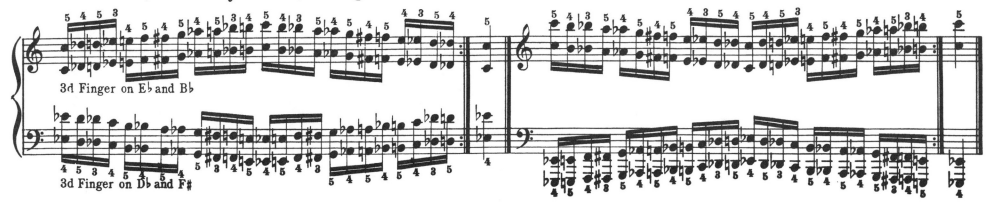

3d Finger on E♭ and B♭

3d Finger on D♭ and F♯

Arpeggios in the Key of C

Common Chord of C Major, in similar and contrary motion

2d Position (1st Inversion) of the Chord of C Major, in similar and contrary motion

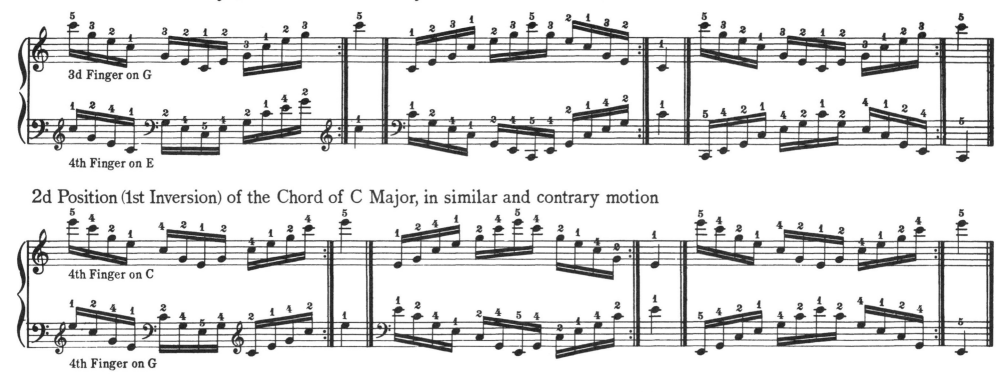

3d Position (2d Inversion) of the Chord of C Major, in similar and contrary motion

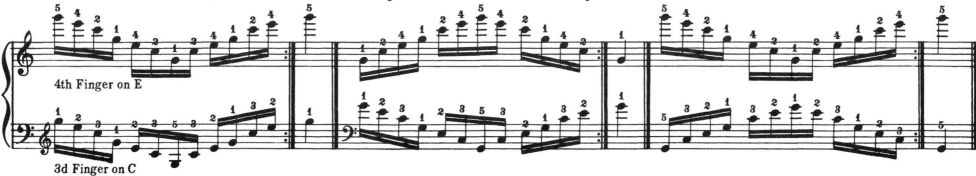

Common Chord of C Minor, in similar and contrary motion

3d Finger on G

4th Finger on E♭

2d Position (1st Inversion) of the Chord of C Minor, in similar and contrary motion

4th Finger on E♭

4th Finger on E♭

3d Position (2d Inversion) of the Chord of C Minor, in similar and contrary motion

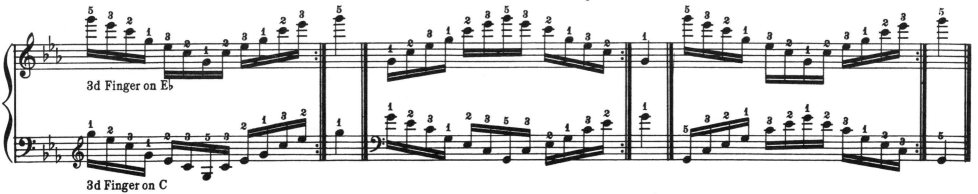

3d Finger on E♭

3d Finger on C

Chord of C Major, in similar motion, from Different Intervals

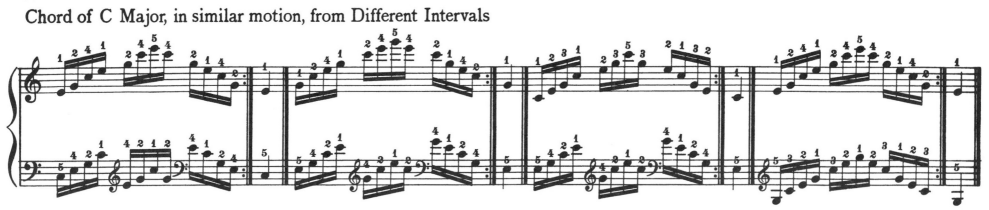

Chord of C Major, in contrary motion, from Different Intervals

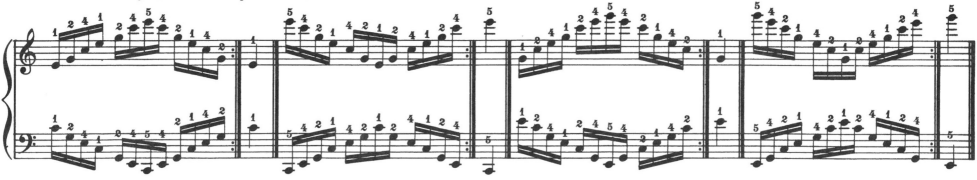

Chord of C Minor, in similar motion, from Different Intervals

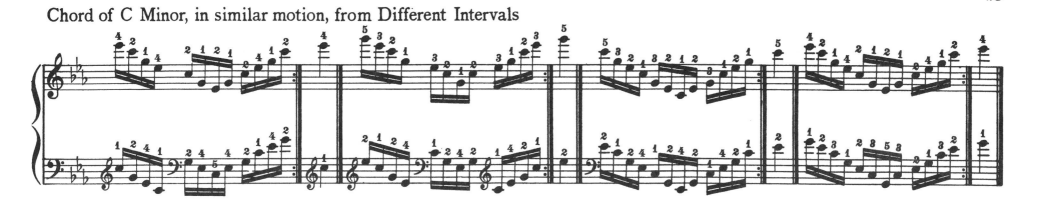

Chord of C Minor, in contrary motion, from Different Intervals

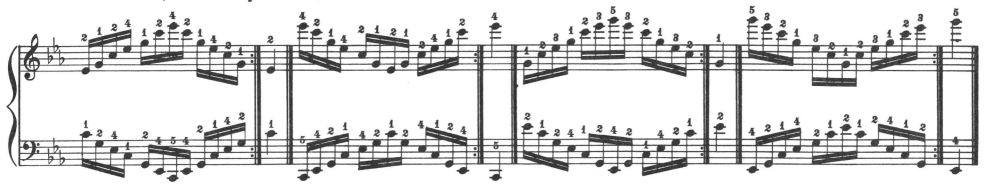

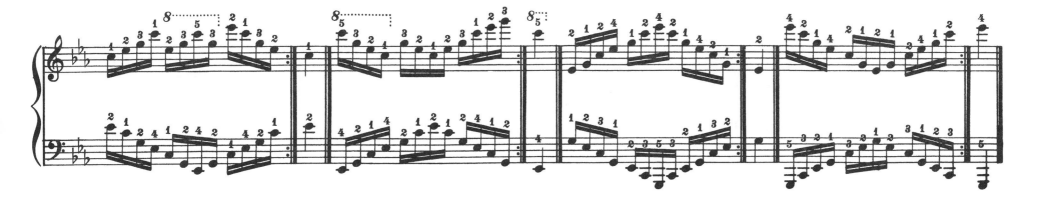

Dominant Seventh-Chord and its Inversions, in similar motion

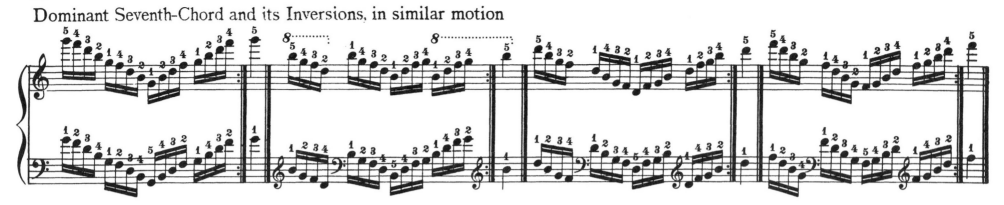

Dominant Seventh-Chord and its Inversions, in contrary motion

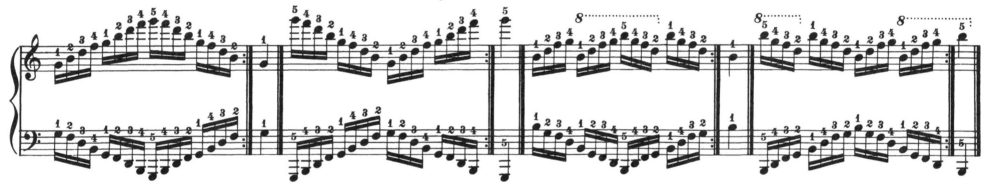

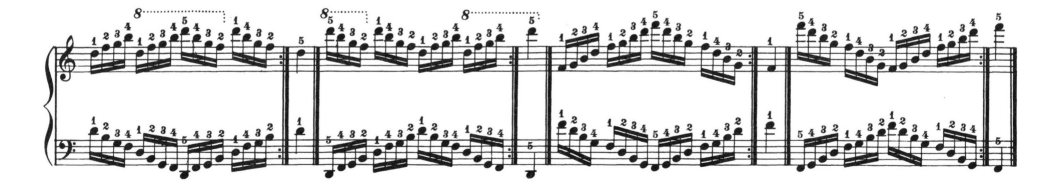

Dominant Seventh-Chord, in similar motion, the hands starting on different notes

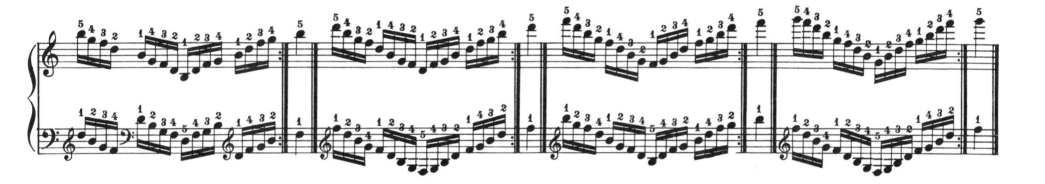

Dominant Seventh-Chord, in contrary motion, the hands starting on different notes

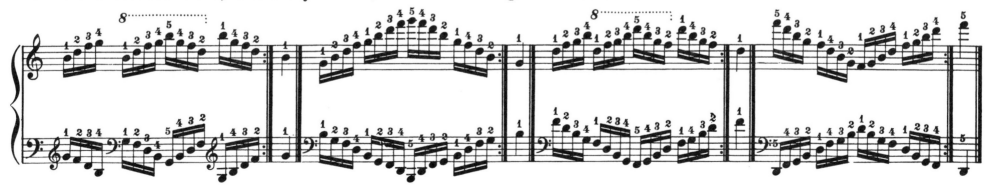

Diminished Seventh-Chord of C major and minor and its inversions, in similar motion

Diminished Seventh-Chord of C major and minor, in contrary motion

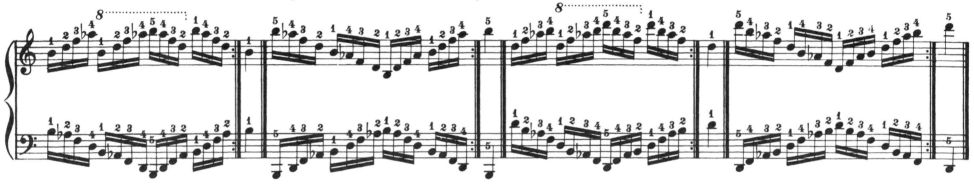

Chord of the Eleventh or Added Sixth (Key of C major and minor), in similar and contrary motion

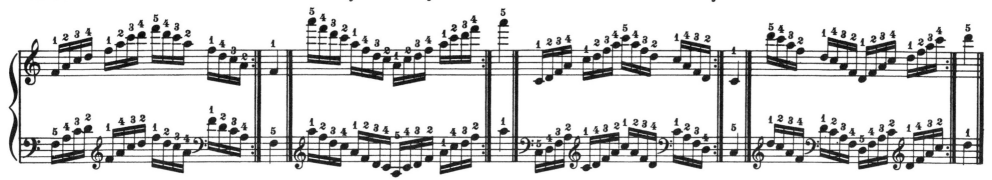

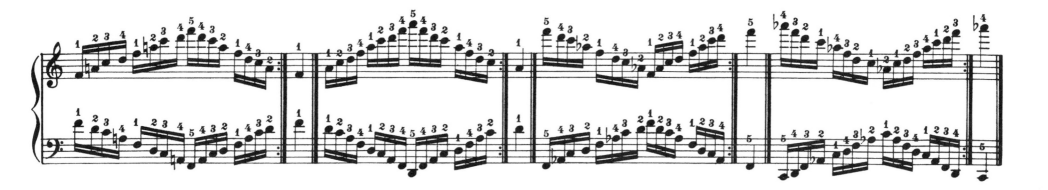

Arbitrary (or Melodic) Minor Scales

In Thirds (or Tenths) and Sixths

C Minor

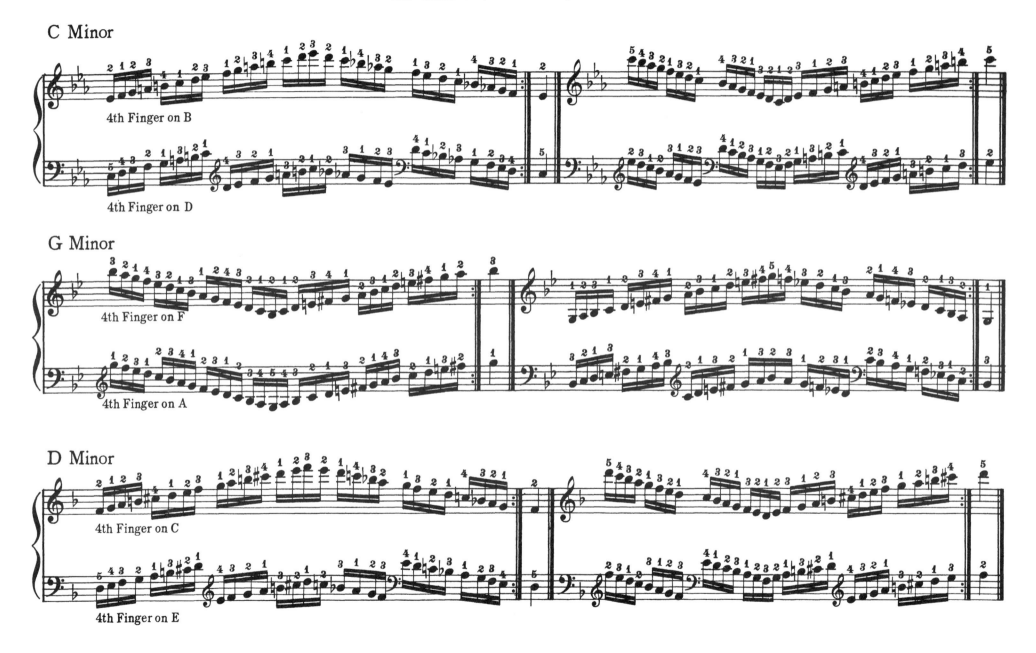

4th Finger on B

4th Finger on D

G Minor

4th Finger on F

4th Finger on A

D Minor

4th Finger on C

4th Finger on E

A Minor

4th Finger on G

4th Finger on B

E Minor

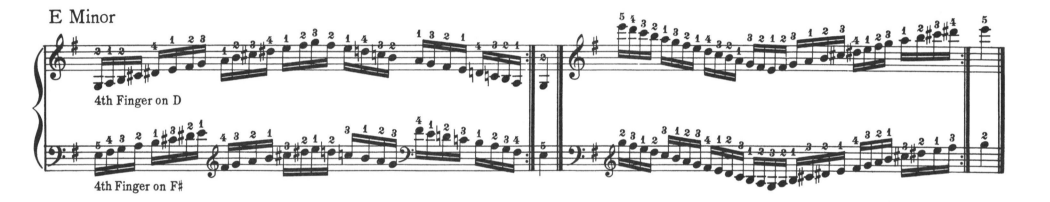

4th Finger on D

4th Finger on F♯

B Minor

4th Finger on A

4th Finger on F♯ and on the initial note

F♯ Minor

4th Finger on D♯ ascending and on G♯ descending

4th Finger on F♯

C♯ Minor

4th Finger on A♯ ascending and on D♯ descending

4th Finger on F♯

G♯ Minor (Enharmonic Equivalent: A♭ Minor)

4th Finger on A♯

4th Finger on C♯ ascending and on F♯ descending

Eb Minor (Enharmonic Equivalent: D# Minor)

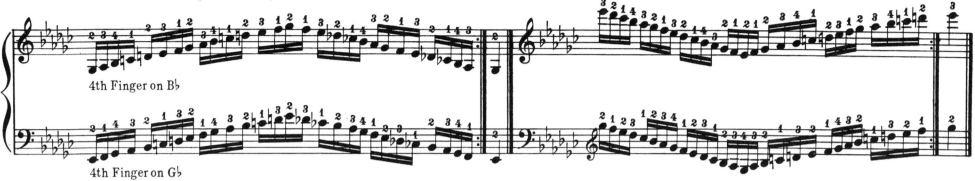

4th Finger on Bb

4th Finger on Gb

Bb Minor

4th Finger on Bb

4th Finger on Gb

F Minor

4th Finger on Bb, and on the highest F

4th Finger on G

25367

Second Appendix

Arpeggios of Common Chords in Close Form

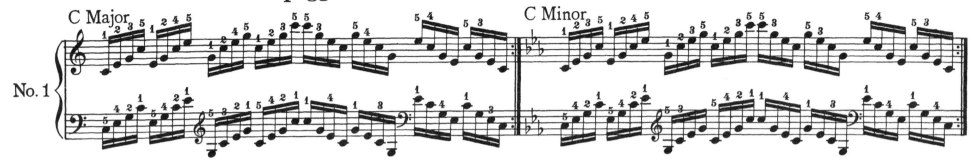

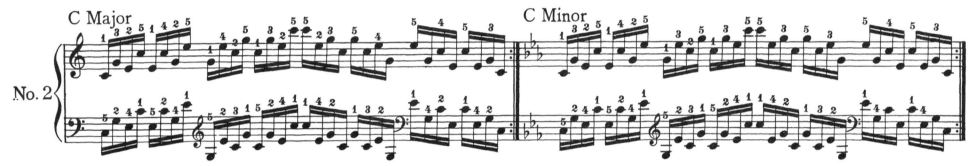

D Major

D Minor

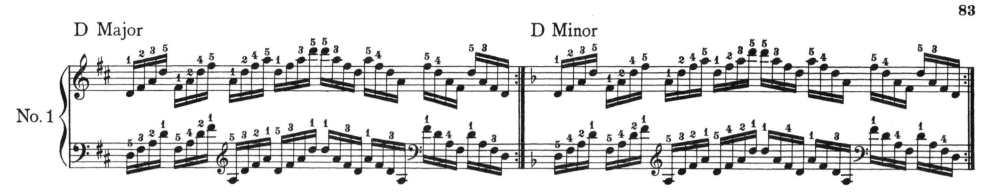

No. 1

D Major

D Minor

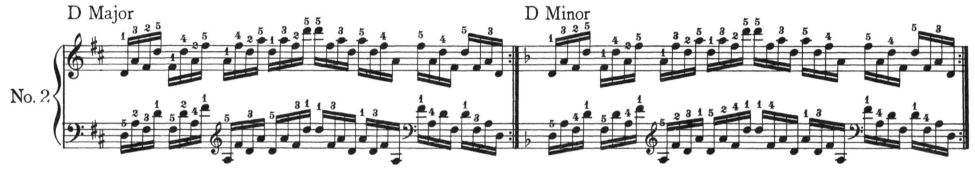

No. 2

A Major

A Minor

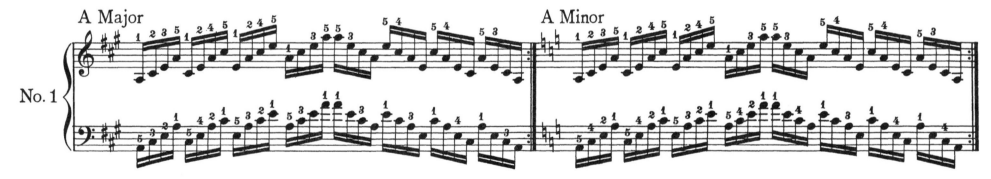

No. 1

A Major

A Minor

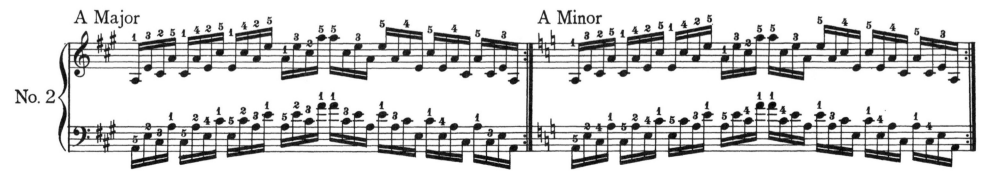

No. 2

E Major

E Minor

E Major

E Minor

No. 2

B Major

B Minor

No. 1

B Major

B Minor

No. 2

F# Major

F# Minor

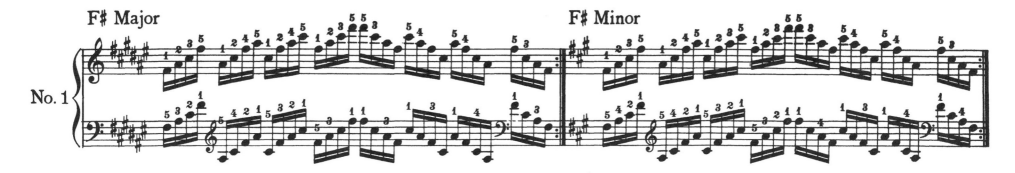

No. 1

F# Major

F# Minor

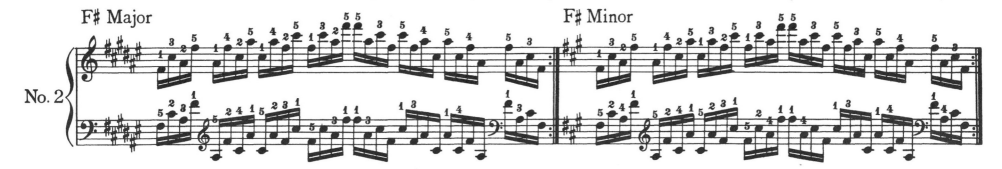

No. 2

C# Major (Enharmonic Equivalent: Db)

C# Minor

No. 1

C# Major

C# Minor

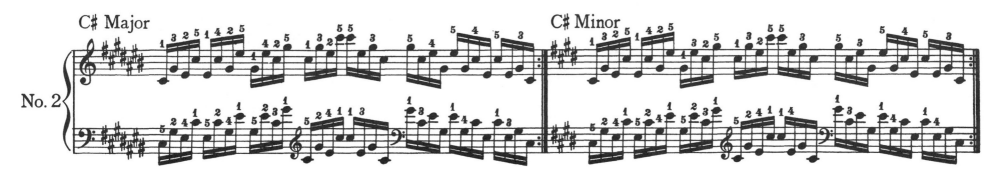

No. 2

25367

Ab Major

Ab Minor (Enharmonic Enquivalent: G# Minor)

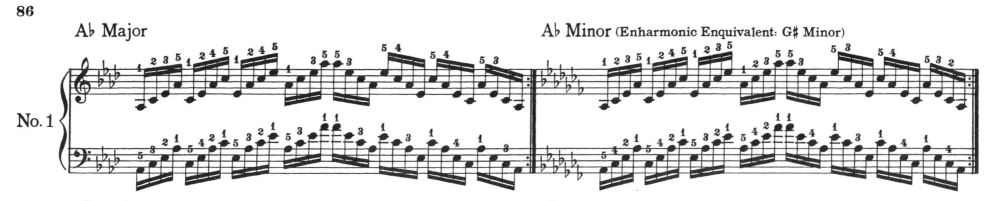

No. 1

Ab Major

Ab Minor

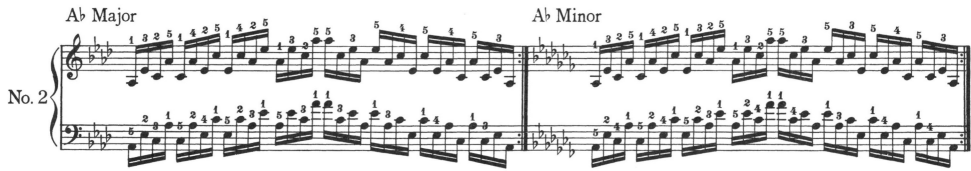

No. 2

Eb Major

Eb Minor

No. 1

Eb Major

Eb Minor

No. 2

Bb Major

Bb Minor

No. 1

Bb Major

Bb Minor

No. 2

F Major

F Minor

No. 1

F Major

F Minor

No. 2

Arpeggios of the Dominant Seventh in Close Form

In the Key of C, Major and Minor

No. 1

No. 2

In the Key of G, Major and Minor

No. 1

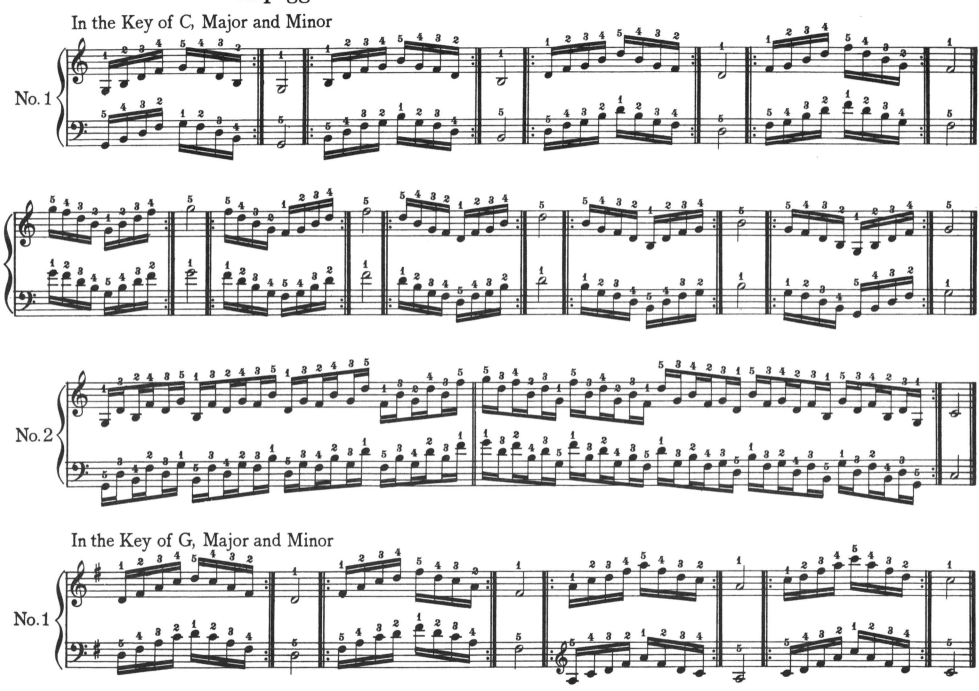

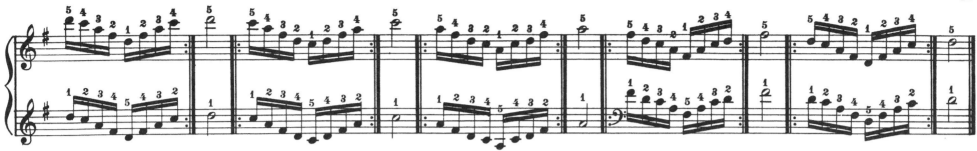

In the Key of D, Major and Minor

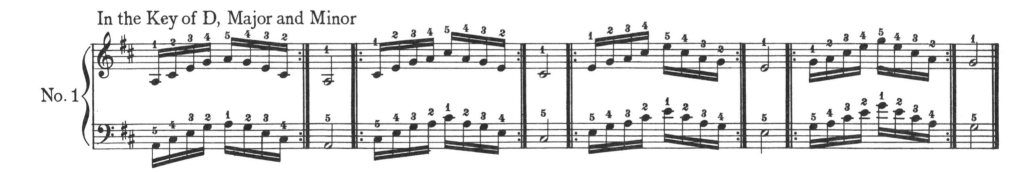

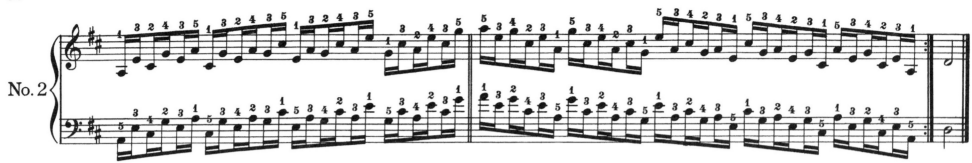

No. 2

In the Key of A, Major and Minor

No. 1

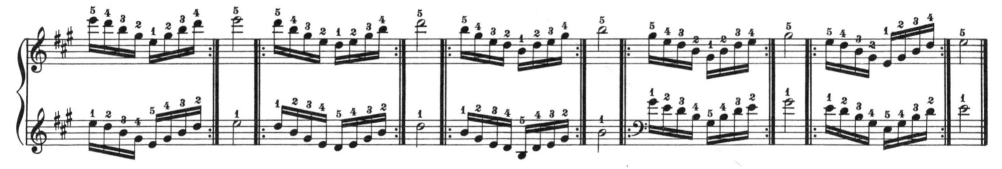

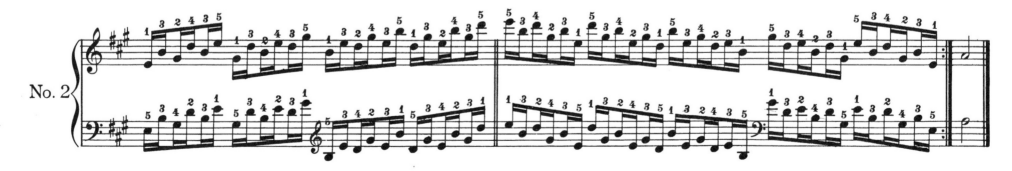

No. 2

In the Key of E, Major and Minor

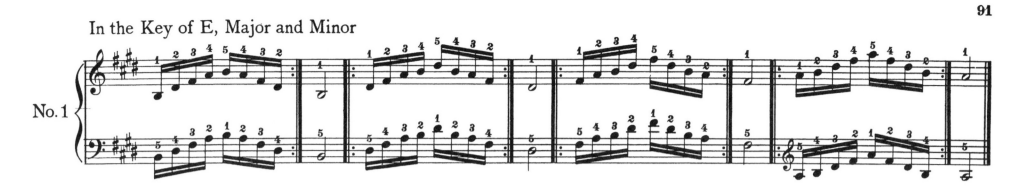

No.1

No.2

In the Key of B, Major and Minor

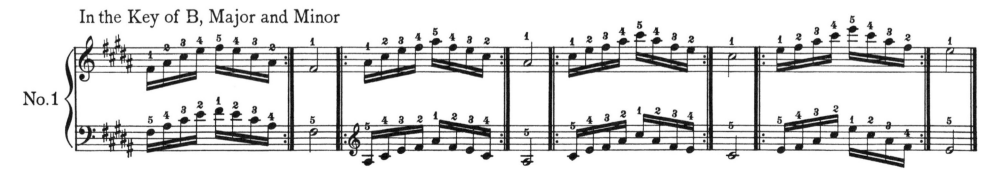

No.1

25367

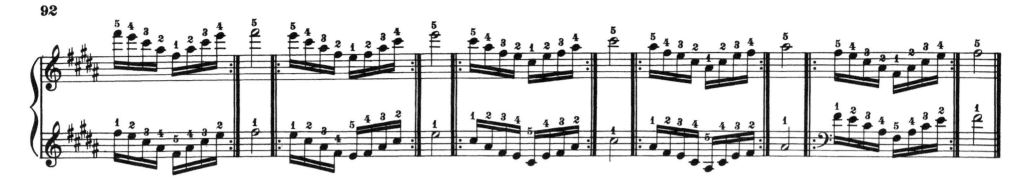

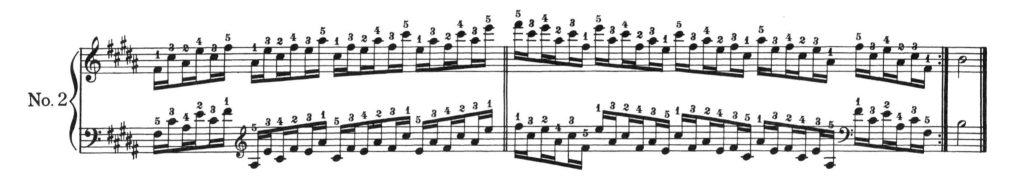

No. 2

In the Key of F♯, Major and Minor

No. 1

No. 2

In the Key of C♯, Major and Minor (Enharmonic Equivalent: D♭)

No. 1

No. 2

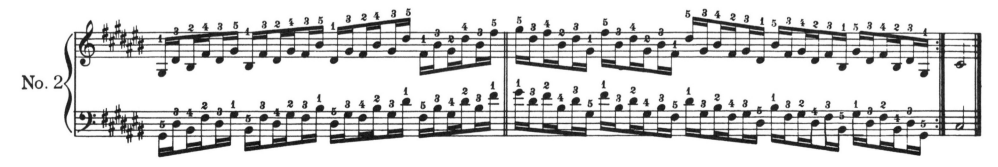

25367

In the Key of A♭, Major and Minor (Enharmonic Equivalent G♯)

No.1

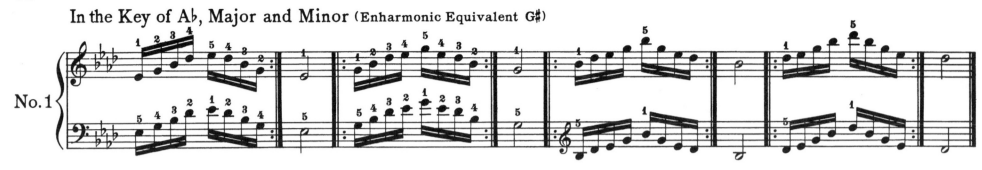

No.2

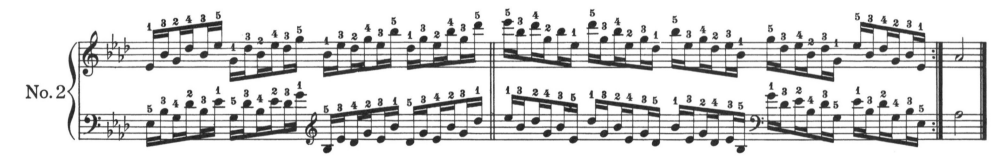

In the Key of E♭, Major and Minor

No.1

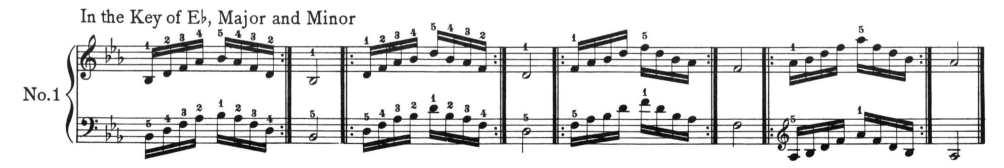

In the Key of B♭, Major and Minor

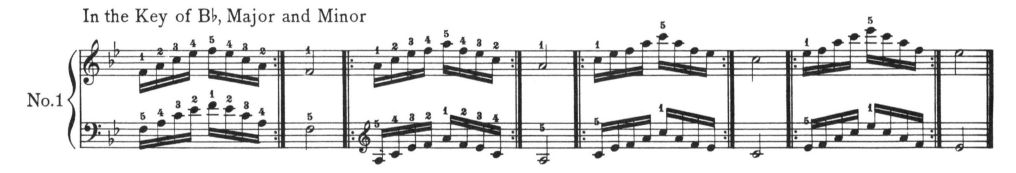

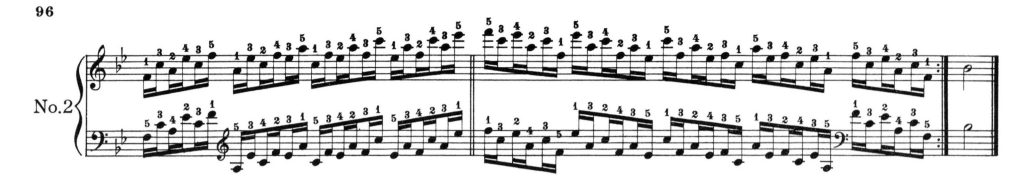

No.2

In the Key of F, Major and Minor

No.1

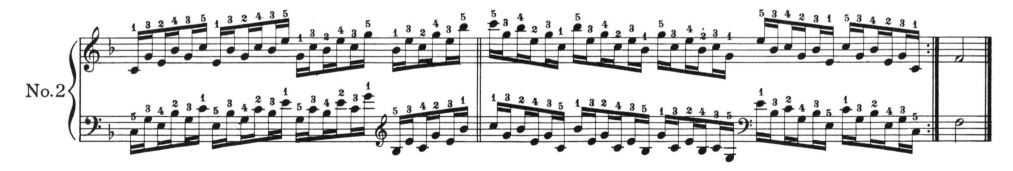

No.2

Arpeggios of Diminished Sevenths in Close Form

In the Key of C, Major and Minor

No. 1

No. 2

In the Key of G, Major and Minor

No. 1

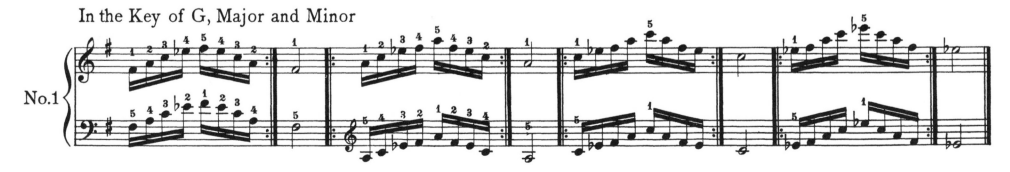

25367

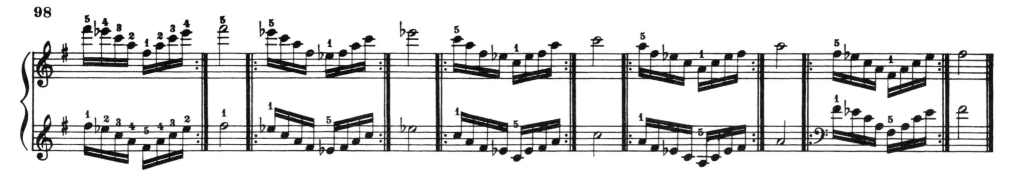

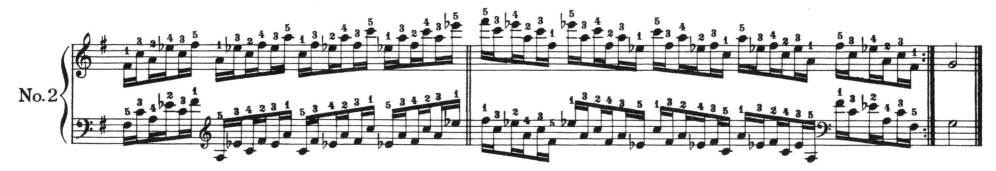

In the Key of D, Major and Minor

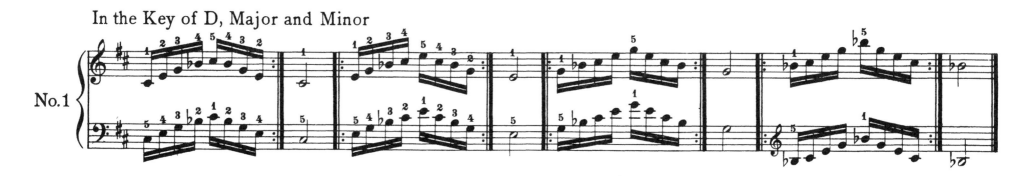

No.2

In the Key of A, Major and Minor

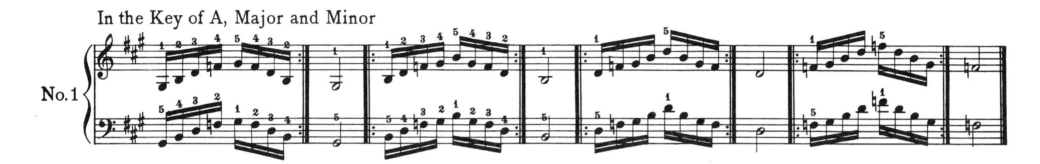

No.1

No.2

25367

In the Key of E, Major and Minor

No.1

No.2

In the Key of B, Major and Minor

No.1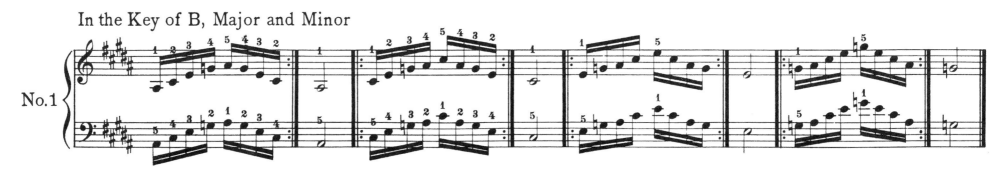

In the Key of F♯, Major and Minor

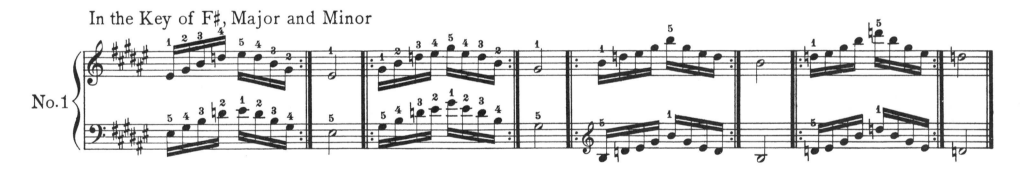

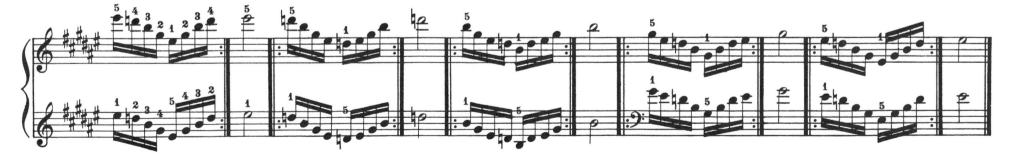

No.2

In the Key of C♯, Major and Minor

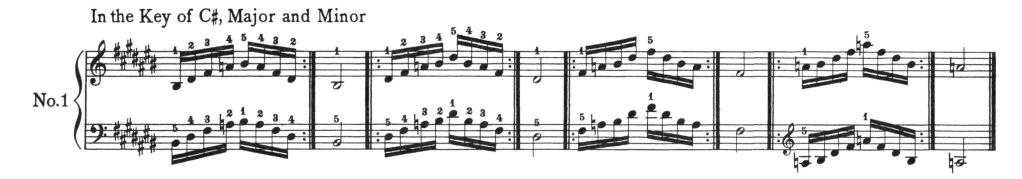

No.1

No.2

In the Key of A♭, Major and Minor

No.1

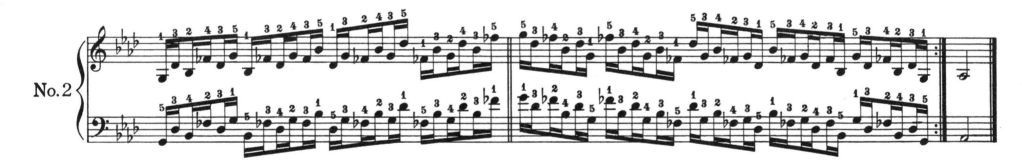

No.2

In the Key of E♭, Major and Minor

No.1

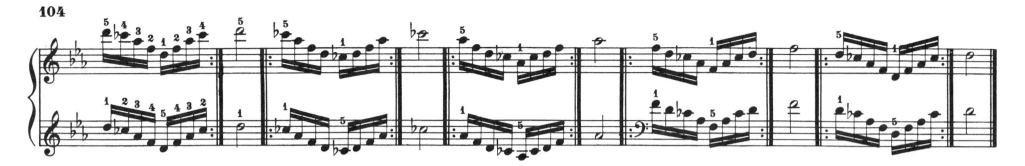

No.2

In the Key of B♭, Major and Minor

No.1

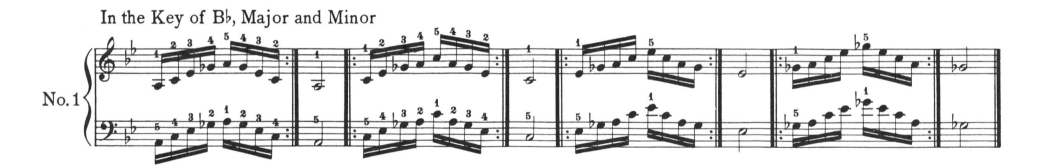

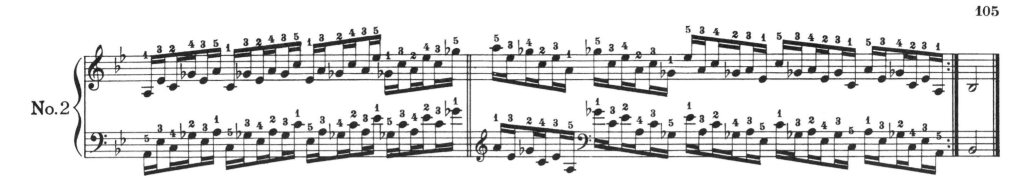

No.2

In the Key of F, Major and Minor

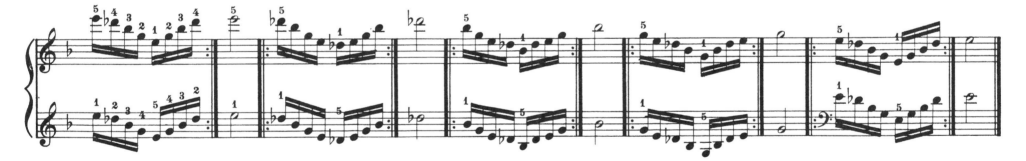

No.1

No.2

The Chromatic Scale in Major Thirds

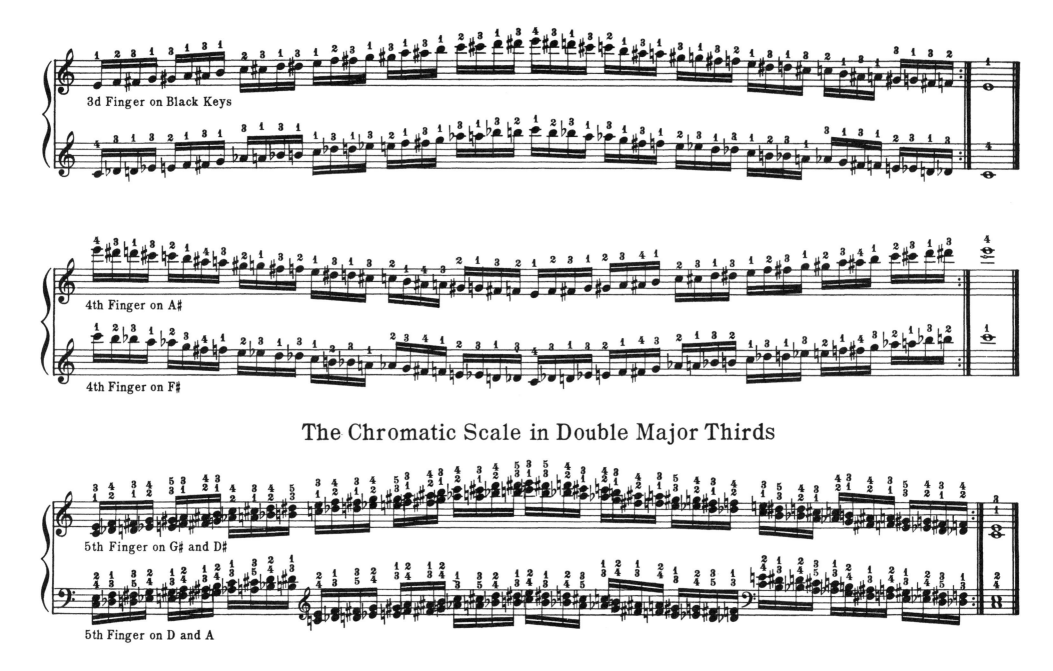

The Chromatic Scale in Double Major Thirds

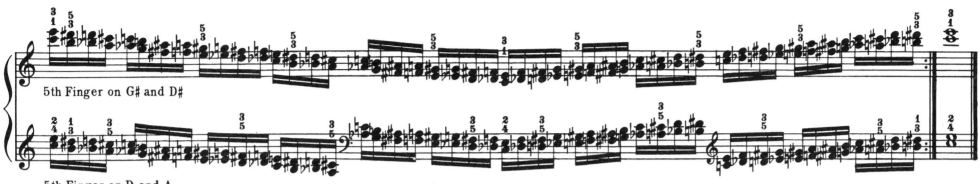

5th Finger on G♯ and D♯

5th Finger on D and A

Chromatic Scale in Double Octaves, a Major Third apart

3d Finger on D♯ and A♯ *(legato)*

3d Finger on F♯ and D♭ *(legato)*

5th Finger and Thumb on every octave, *staccato*, in both hands

SCHIRMER'S LIBRARY
of Musical Classics

SERIES ONE

PIANO METHODS, STUDIES, AND EXERCISES

BERENS, H.

L. 1070	Op. 61.	School of Velocity. 40 Studies. Complete. The Same. L. 259, Bk. ĭ; L. 260, Bk. II; L. 262, Bk. III.
L. 504	Op. 70.	50 Pieces without Octaves. For Beginners.
L. 508	Op. 79.	20 Children—Studies without Octaves.
L. 526	Op. 88.	The School of Scales, Chords, and Embellishments. 28 Studies.
L. 1031	Op. 89.	Training of the Left Hand. 40 Exercises and 25 Studies.

BERTINI, H.

L. 137	Op. 29.	24 Studies, Preparatory to the Cramer Studies (Vogrich-Buonamici).
L. 138	Op. 32.	24 Studies. A sequel to Op. 29. (Vogrich-Buonamici).
L. 136	Op. 100.	25 Easy Studies. (Vogrich-Buonamici).
L. 758	Op. 101.	24 Melodious Pieces.
L. 795		50 Selected Studies from Op. 100, 29, and 32. (Germer).
L. 691	Op. 166.	25 Primary Etudes. (Osterle).
L. 1588		50 Selected Studies from Op. 29, 32, 100, 134 (Buonamici-Cornell). Bk. I; L. 1589, Bk. II. sp. e.

BIEHL, A.

L. 530	Op. 30.	The Elements of Piano-Playing.
L. 497	Op. 44.	25 Easy and Progressive Studies. With special reference to the left hand. Bk. I; L. 498, Bk. II.

BRAHMS, J.

L. 1600	51 Exercises.

BRAUER, F.

L. 494	Op. 15.	12 Studies for Development of Velocity.

BURGMULLER, F.

L. 500	Op. 100.	25 Easy and Progressive Studies. (Oesterle). Complete. The Same. L. 977, Bk. I; L. 978, Bk. II.
L. 755	Op. 105.	12 Brilliant and Melodious Studies. (Oesterle).
L. 752	Op. 109.	18 Characteristic Studies (Oesterle).

CHOPIN, F.

L. 1551	Etudes (Mikuli).
L. 33	Etudes (Friedheim.)

CLEMENTI, M.

L. 167	Gradus ad Parnassum. 100 Exercises. (Vogrich). Bk. I; L. 168, Bk. II.
L. 780	Gradus ad Parnassum. 29 Selected Studies. (Tausig).
L. 1112	The Same. sp. f. e.
L. 376	Preludes and Exercises in all the Major and Minor Keys. (Vogrich).

CONCONE, G.

L. 139	Op. 24.	25 Melodic Studies. (Oesterle).
L. 141	Op. 25.	15 Studies in Style and Expression. (Oesterle).
L. 140	Op. 30.	20 Studies on the Singing Touch. (Oesterle).
L. 1374	Op. 31.	15 Studies in Style. (Deis).
L. 226	Op. 37.	24 Brilliant Preludes in all the Major and Minor Keys. For Small Hands.
L. 1030	Op. 44.	15 Studies in Expression. (von Doenhoff).
L. 25		30 Selected Studies. (Oesterle).

CRAMER, J. B.

L. 142	84 Studies. Bk. I.; L. 143, Bk. II.; L. 144, Bk. III.; L. 145, Bk. IV.
L. 827	50 Selected Studies. (Bulow). Complete.
L. 828	The Same. L. 828, Bk. I.; L. 829, Bk. II.; L. 830, Bk. III.; L. 831, Bk. IV.
L. 1178	The Same. L. 1178. Complete. sp.

CROISEZ, A.

L. 1438	Op. 100.	25 Melodious Etudes. (Deis).

CZERNY, C.

L. 153	Op. 139.	100 Progressive Studies without Octaves. (Vogrich).
L. 378	Op. 261.	125 Exercises in Passage-Playing. Elementary Studies. (Buonamici).
L. 161	Op. 299.	The School of Velocity. 40 Studies. (Vogrich). Complete. The Same. L. 162, Bk. I.; L. 163, Bk. II.; L. 164, Bk. III.; L. 165, Bk. IV.
L. 150	Op. 335.	The School of Legato and Staccato. 50 Studies. Sequel to Op. 299. (Buonamici).
L. 149	Op. 337.	40 Daily Exercises. (Buonamici).
L. 383	Op. 365.	School of the Virtuoso. Studies in bravura and style. (Buonamici).
L. 749	Op. 453.	110 Easy and Progressive Exercises. (Buonamici).
L. 402	Op. 553.	6 Octave Studies in Progressive Difficulty. (Schultze).
L. 146	Op. 599.	Practical Method for Beginners. (Buonamici).
L. 148	Op. 636.	Preliminary School of Finger Dexterity. (Buonamici).
L. 60	Op. 718.	24 Studies for the Left Hand. (Scharfenburg).
L. 154	Op. 740.	The Art of Finger Dexterity. 50 Studies in Brilliant Style. (Vogrich). Complete. The Same. L. 155, Bk. I.; L. 156, Bk. II.; L. 157, Bk. III.; L. 158, Bk. IV.; L. 159, Bk. V.; L. 160, Bk. VI.
L. 1158	Op. 755.	Perfection in Style. 25 Finishing Studies. (Herzog).
L. 192	Op. 802.	Practical Finger Exercises. (Relle). Complete.
L. 147	Op. 821.	160 Eight-Measure Exercises. (Buonamici).
L. 54	Op. 823.	The Little Pianist. 75 Exercises, beginning with the First Rudiments. Complete. The Same. L. 55, Bk. I.; L. 56, Bk. II.
L. 272	Op. 849.	30 New Studies in Technics. Preparatory to Op. 299. (Buonamici).
L. 994		Selected Studies. An Anthology. (Oesterle). Bk. I: Upper Elementary and Lower Grades. L. 995, Bk. II: Middle Grades. L. 996, Bk. III: Upper and Middle Grades. L. 997, Bk. IV: Upper and Advanced Grades.
L. 445		First Instruction in Piano-Playing. 100 Recreations. (Ruthardt).

G. SCHIRMER, Inc.

DISTRIBUTED BY
HAL·LEONARD

A–1173

DESIGN COPYRIGHT 1939, RENEWED 1967, BY G. SCHIRMER, INC.

SCHIRMER'S LIBRARY of Musical Classics

PIANO METHODS, STUDIES, AND EXERCISES

SERIES TWO

DESIGN COPYRIGHT 1939. RENEWED 1967. BY G. SCHIRMER, INC.

A 1174

DORING, C. H.
L. 651 Op. 24. Exercises and Studies in Staccato Octave-Playing.
L. 1035 Op. 25. 8 Octave Studies.

DUVERNOY, J. B.
L. 316 Op. 120. The School of Mechanism. 15 Studies preparatory to Czerny's "School of Velocity." (Klauser). Complete.
L. 1292 Op. 120. The same: Bk. I.
L. 50 Op. 176. Ecole Primaire. 25 Elementary Studies.

GERMER, H.
L. 1279 Rhythmical Problems.

GURLITT, C.
L. 798 Op. 50. 24 Easy Melodious Studies.
L. 801 Op. 51. 24 Melodious Studies of Medium Difficulty.
L. 534 Op. 82. The First Steps of the Young Pianist. Bk. I.
L. 535 Op. 82. The same: Bk. II.
L. 536 Op. 83. The Easiest Studies in Velocity.
L. 807 Op. 85. 24 Studies on Scales and Arpeggios.
L. 539 Op. 100. 24 Octave Studies.
L. 323 Op. 107. Buds and Blossoms. 12 Melodious Studies.
L. 324 Op. 117. The First Lessons.
L. 339 Op. 130. 35 Easy Studies without Octaves.
L. 206 Op. 131. 24 Melodious and Progressive Studies.
L. 326 Op. 141. School of Velocity. 24 Short Studies for Beginners.

HABERBIER, E.
L. 191 Op. 53. Etudes-Poesies. (Ruthardt).
Op. 59.

HANDROCK, J.
L. 925 Mechanical Studies.

HANON, C. L.
L. 299 The Virtuoso Pianist in 60 Exercises.

HELLER, S.
L. 179 Op. 16. The Art of Phrasing. 26 Melodious Studies, Bk. I.
L. 180 Op. 16. The same: Bk. II.
L. 176 Op. 45. 25 Melodious Studies. Complete.
L. 1117 Op. 45. The same: Bk. I.
L. 177 Op. 46. 30 Progressive Studies. Complete.
L. 1120 Op. 46. The same: Bk. I.
L. 178 Op. 47. 25 Studies for Rhythm and Expression. Complete.
L. 1123 Op. 47. The same: Bk. I.
L. 130 Op. 81. 24 Preludes.
L. 748 Op. 119. 32 Preludes. (Oesterle).
L. 766 Op. 125. 24 Studies for Rhythm and Expression. (Scharfenberg).
L. 24 50 Selected Studies from Op. 45, 46, 47. (Oesterle).

HENSELT, A.
L. 44 Op. 2. 12 Characteristic Concert-Studies. (Jonas).

HERZ, H.
L. 170 Scales and Exercises. (Vogrich).
L. 1083 The same: sp. e.

JENSEN, A.
L. 763 Op. 32. 25 Etudes. Bk. I.
L. 764 Op. 32. The same: Bk. II.
L. 765 Op. 32. The same: Bk. III.

KESSLER, J. C.
L. 1416 Op. 20. 15 Selected Studies. (Deis).

KOHLER, L.
L. 317 Op. 50. First Studies. (Klauser).
L. 543 Op. 60. 20 Studies in Continuous Scale-and-Chord Passages.
L. 318 Op. 151. 12 Easiest Studies.
L. 425 Op. 157. 12 Easy Studies. (Klauser).
L. 196 Op. 163. 16 Elementary Studies.
L. 480 Op. 190. The Very Easiest Studies.
L. 321 Op. 242. Short School of Velocity without Octaves.
L. 1082 Op. 249. Metodo Practico. sp. e, Bk. I.
L. 935 Op. 300. Practical Method. (Oesterle). Bk. I.
L. 936 Op. 300. The same: Bk. II.

KRAUSE, A.
L. 481 School of Etudes, Bk. I: Lower Elementary Grade.
L. 482 The same: Bk. II. Elementary Grade.
L. 483 The same: Bk. III. Lower Medium Grade.

KUHNER, C.
L. 553 Op. 2. 10 Trill Studies.

KULLAK, T.
L. 475 Op. 48. The School of Octave-Playing. Bk. I: Preliminary School.
L. 476 Op. 48. The same: Bk. II: 7 Octave Studies.

KUNZ, K. M.
L. 939 Op. 14. 200 Short Two-Part Canons. For the Beginner.

LE CARPENTIER, A.
L. 1133 A Piano Method for Children. sp. e.

LE COUPPEY, F.
L. 430 Op. 17. The Alphabet. 25 Very Easy Studies. (Scharfenberg).
L. 67 Op. 20. L'Agilité. 25 Progressive Studies for Mechanism and Light Touch.
L. 63 Op. 96. 15 Preparatory Studies to Czerny's "School of Velocity".

LEMOINE, H.
L. 175 Op. 37. Etudes Enfantines. (Scharfenberg).

LISZT, F.
L. 835 6 Grand Etudes after N. Paganini. (Gallico).
L. 788 12 Etudes d'exécution transcendante. (Gallico).

G. SCHIRMER, Inc.

DISTRIBUTED BY HAL•LEONARD